How to Cope
When You Can't

HOW TO
COPE
WHEN YOU CAN'T

A How-to Guide to Help You Cope With the Stress of Modern Living

DR. DON GOSSETT

HUNTINGTON  HOUSE INC.

Lafayette, Louisiana 70508

Huntington House, Inc.
1200 N. Market St., Shreveport, LA 71107

Library of Congress Catalog Card Number
85-82556

ISBN Number 0-910311-35-8

Designed by Koechel-Peterson
Layout and typesetting by Publications Technologies

Printed in the United States of America

Contents

Introduction

Coping. Every day we are told we must cope with one problem after another. Rebellious children. Financial difficulties. Stress. Divorce. Sickness.

Satan seems to be working overtime to bring panic and pain to God's people. Shackled by an ignorance of their privileges in Christ, many Christians are shortchanged by the devil. Blindly they accept whatever woes Satan hurls at them. They passively adopt a "woe-is-me" attitude and merely endure life when they could be enjoying it.

I have good news for you! You don't need to stumble through life in the blindness of unbelief. Instead, you can stride forward in faith, aglow with the presence of God burning in your soul, to overcome every obstacle the devil places in your way.

That is why I have written this book: to show you *How to Cope When You Can't*. In its pages we deal with more than 20 of the most common problems people are confronted with today including:

How to Cope with Financial Difficulties
How to Cope with Stress

5

How to Cope with Depression
How to Cope with an Inferiority Complex
How to Cope with Sickness
How to Cope with Sorrow
How to Cope with Fear
How to Cope with Unmet Needs

Through the Word of God we not only tell you how to cope with each of these problems, but also how to conquer them in the all-powerful Name of our Lord Jesus Christ.

Dr. Don Gossett
Box G1
Blaine, WA 98230

In Canada:
Dr. Don Gossett
White Rock, British Columbia
Canada V4B 5G4

Chapter One

How to Cope
When You Can't

Some people may be reading this book because they read some other book of mine, and liked it. Others will be reading it because they've heard me on radio, or seen me on TV. But some people will be reading this book because of its title: *How to Cope When You Can't.*

If there is a problem you can't cope with, I have good news for you: coping is not a do-it-yourself proposition. There is a God in heaven. He does work miracles today, and those miracles are available to all of His children.

I have seen some big problems in my life — and God has blessed me with some big solutions.

Our third child, Jeanne Michelle, was born with club-feet. God healed her.

My wife, Joyce, nearly died with rheumatic fever. God healed her too.

Again and again, God has provided the finances our family has needed, just when our family needed them — even when I was a traveling evangelist with no regular source of income.

7

I have seen God move in other people's lives to open blind eyes, heal cancer, and deliver them from drugs, alcohol, arthritis, mental torment — all sorts of afflictions.

The more I see of God's power, the more I am convinced that there is only one way to cope when YOU can't cope, and that's by tapping into the supernatural power of God through prayer. Jesus taught us clearly that we can survive the Christian life only by maintaining a constant life of prayer. He declared, "Men ought always to pray, and not to faint" (Luke 18:1). I have heard two striking translations of this verse: "Men ought always to pray, and not to cave in." Again, "Men ought always to pray, and not to turn out badly."

There will be no fainting, no caving in, no turning out badly, if we maintain a life of prayer.

In the fall of the first year Joyce and I were married, we journeyed down to the Gulf of Mexico. For four weeks we conducted meetings at the Cedar Bayou Assembly of God Church in Baytown, Texas. The meetings concluded in mid-November, and we had nothing more scheduled until January.

Baytown is only a short drive from Houston, Texas, and I wanted to meet the famous evangelist, Raymond T. Ritchie, who, with his brother's help, was then pastoring Houston's Evangelistic Temple.

I drove into Houston to meet Brother Ritchie. As I traveled down the highway, my mind was rehearsing many things about this man of God. He had used a huge, red, white, and blue tent during World War II to conduct meetings that shook cities for God's glory.

During those war years, Brother Ritchie had ministered nightly to thousands of people.

When I met him, he was most gracious. We had a blessed time of sharing together and I felt privileged to be in his presence. Here I was, 21 years old and a novice in the ministry. And there was Raymond T. Ritchie, a seasoned man of God, in his sixties. He was a vibrant, cheerful man.

After a couple of hours of fellowship, Brother Ritchie made a suggestion: "Since you don't have any meetings scheduled for the next six weeks, why don't you come and work with me here at the Temple? I will pay you $25 a week to help you financially, and you can just be my constant companion in all phases of the ministry."

I agreed gladly to his proposal. The next six weeks were a real learning experience for me. I was being personally tutored by one of God's generals of the faith.

The most impressive characteristic of Brother Ritchie was his prayer life. I learned firsthand the meaning of Romans 12:12 "... continuing constant in prayer ..."

In my association with this man in his daily round of duties, there were many cases of counseling, urgent phone messages, problems both large and small. Always, without fail, Raymond T. Ritchie interpreted these matters as a call to prayer. Seldom did I see him on his knees talking with God. But as he performed his ministerial duties, he was praying constantly.

To give you a living example of how he performed this beautiful duty of prayer, I recall the morning I walked in and shared with him some important news: "Brother Ritchie, my wife, Joyce, went to the doctor yesterday, and it was confirmed that we are expecting our first baby."

Immediately he grasped my hand and began to pray for Joyce, for the unborn baby, for health for both of them, for a normal delivery, and that our baby would grow up to love and serve the Lord!

I know Raymond T. Ritchie had his seasons alone with the Lord in protracted times of prayer: it was obvious by his whole attitude. But I was deeply inspired by his method of "instant communication with God." Brother Ritchie felt that every situation that arose was something to pray about.

He told me one day, "When we are commanded to 'pray without ceasing,' that's not always done on our knees. But as we walk, drive, counsel, make decisions ... everything is to be bathed in prayer."

Raymond T. Ritchie prayed because he knew the power of prayer. When he ran into a problem, he didn't try to cope with it on his own. He didn't go through life as a "do-it-yourselfer." Like any pastor, he had hurting people and heartbreaking problems to face on a regular basis: bereaved parents, sick people, ailing marriages, broken homes, the poor, the so-called "incurably" ill. These people didn't want sympathy; they didn't want slogans; they wanted solutions. And Brother Ritchie knew where to go to find them.

If you are not yet a believer — or you attend a church which does not teach the miracle-working power of God — you may find the idea of praying about your problems a little far-fetched.

"God helps those who help themselves," you're probably thinking.

Did you know that "God helps those who help themselves" isn't in the Bible? If you want to know what God will and won't do, the only reliable source of information is the Bible — the Word of God. According to that Word, "God is our refuge and strength, a very present help in trouble" (Psalm 46:1).

One of the most fascinating true stories I've ever read is that of Roberta Lashley Bonnici, of Lexington Park, Maryland. Her story appeared in the December, 1965, issue of *Guideposts* magazine, read by millions. She has given me permission to reprint this account:

> The prayer session at our church that Friday night was such a fine one that I let nine p.m. slip by, only vaguely aware that now I'd have to wait until 11:20 for the next bus. It was ten minutes before midnight when the bus let me out on the lonely country road, still a 20-minute walk from home.
>
> Ordinarily I disliked this steep climb to our house on Bald Knob Road. But tonight I was still in the spell of the prayer meeting, buoyed up with the idealistic thoughts of a 17-year-old in the first flush of belief.
>
> It was not until a car drew up beside me on the dark road that I realized I was tired. "How about a lift?" a man's voice asked as the door

swung open. I climbed gratefully in and only then realized that the driver was a stranger — not a neighbor as I'd thought. In our rural neighborhood, sharing rides was such an accepted practice that no slightest warning crossed my mind as I thanked the driver. He did not reply to my thanks and so we drove in silence until I pointed out my house. There was no decrease in speed. "That's my house," I repeated. Was it my imagination or were we going even faster? We passed the house. "There's a lane ahead where you can turn," I told him, trying to keep panic from my voice.

There was no mistaking it now: the car was gaining speed, careening crazily up the twisting mountain road. The last house was behind us now. "Stop the car!" I cried. "Let me out!" Without slowing, the car swerved up a bumpy side road that led to an abandoned coal mine high on the mountain. I looked wildly at the trees whizzing past us. A person could be killed and hidden forever in one of those deserted shafts. My hand closed on the door handle. And as it did, I suddenly remembered something I had heard at the Friday night service several weeks before. A missionary to the Philippines had talked about evil spirits. He said that Christians had authority to rebuke these powers in Jesus' name.

Shutting my eyes, I tried to remember the exact words the missionary had used. Then, very slowly and clearly, addressing the evil intent within the man, I said:

"I rebuke you in the Name of Jesus Christ."

For the first time the man looked at me. "What do you mean?" he said. "What's rebuke?"

"I mean," I said, trying to keep my voice steady, "that Jesus Christ has absolute authority on this earth and that I am under His protection."

We had reached the mine. The car stopped. Time stopped, too, as I felt my pulse pounding. The driver sat motionless, hands still on the wheel. "I didn't know," he said at last.

Suddenly I realized that we were backing up, then moving down the steep mine road toward the main road. The crisis was past: waves of relief swept over me.

"I'm really not so bad," the man went on as he headed the car down the mountain. He sounded almost pleading. "I've been to church. It just never made any sense to me."

I don't know if I made sense either, but in the five minutes it took to reach my house, I poured out my heart-felt conviction of Christ's love for each of us and our need for Him.

The car stopped at our driveway and I walked trembling into the house. Mother was waiting for me. "God took care of me," was all I could tell her. "God took care of me," over and over again like a child waking up from a nightmare.

I never saw the car or the man again. I never knew if the words God gave me to say to him were the ones he needed for his own soul's torment. I know only that for me the psalmist's words ring with special joy:

"He only is my rock and my salvation; He is my defense" (Psalm 62:6).

RX for Action:

Are there situations in your life that you have been unable to decide how to handle? Things you really don't know how to handle? Problems that it will take a miracle to resolve? There is only One Person who can work miracles, but He's available: take your problems to Him in prayer.

God Answers Prayer

Throughout this book, you will read Scriptures that reveal without any room for doubt that God will answer when you pray. Here are just a few of the Bible promises you can count on:

And call upon me in the day of trouble: I will deliver thee, and thou shalt glorify me.

PSALM 50:15

As for me, I will call upon God; and the LORD shall save me. Evening, and morning, and at noon, will I pray, and cry aloud: and he shall hear my voice.

PSALM 55:16, 17

Because he hath set his love upon me, therefore will I deliver him: I will set him on high, because he hath known my name. He shall call upon me, and I will answer him: I will be with him in trouble; I will deliver him, and honour him. With long life will I satisfy him, and shew him my salvation.

PSALM 91:14-16

Then shalt thou call, and the LORD shall answer; thou shalt cry, and he shall say, Here I am.

ISAIAH 58:9

And it shall come to pass, that before they call, I will answer; and while they are yet speaking, I will hear.

ISAIAH 65:24

Ask, and it shall be given you; seek, and ye shall find; knock, and it shall be opened unto you: For every one that asketh receiveth; and he that seeketh findeth; and to him that knocketh it shall be opened.

MATTHEW 7:7, 8

Again I say unto you, That if two of you shall agree on earth as touching any thing that they shall ask, it shall be done for them of my Father which is in heaven.

MATTHEW 18:19

If ye shall ask any thing in my name, I will do it.
                                        JOHN 14:14

But without faith it is impossible to please him: for
he that cometh to God must believe that he is, and that he
is a rewarder of them that diligently seek him.
                                        HEBREWS 11:6

Chapter Two

How I Began to Cope

Most of my life has been a struggle to cope with difficult circumstances. Early in my Christian walk, I memorized these words: "I can do all things through Christ which strengtheneth me" Philippians 4:13. These ten words have become my motto and have given me the ability to cope with seemingly impossible situations.

First, there was my earnest endeavor to cope with the drinking problem of my father. Robert Edward Gossett was basically a good, hard-working man who loved his family. But his love for the bottle created more problems for his family than his sobriety could recompense. My earliest memories are of Dad's drinking — and of the heartaches it brought to my mother, my sister, my brother, and me.

Just a few days ago, I went back to my old hometown where my Dad was most notorious for his lifestyle. In my quest for "something better" than my Dad and his family experienced, I had turned to Jesus Christ and accepted His salvation at the age of 12. The difficulties I experienced at home had crushed my spirit, and I can still remember how difficult it was for a timid

boy of 12 to cope with the identification of being "Bob
Gossett's boy" while trying to maintain a Christian
testimony.

When I turned 13, I decided I would do my best to
follow on with the Lord. I had heard people talk about
being baptized in water and joining the church. Since I
had received no religious training at home I had no
understanding of what these two steps entailed, but I
was eager to try anything that would help me in my
attempt to be an all-out Christian.

The only person in authority that I knew in that
church was a deacon named Jess Drake. It was to Mr.
Drake I went one Sunday night.

"Mr. Drake," I said hesitantly, "I would like to be
baptized in water. I don't understand all that it means,
but I would like to be baptized. Also, I heard them talk
about joining the church. How could I do that?"

To ask these big questions was a milestone for me.
But now I had done it, and I waited for Mr. Drake to
respond.

Mr. Drake studied my face for a few moments
without answering a word. The longer he waited to say
something, the more overwhelmed I felt about all of this.
After all, there had never been a Christian Gossett
before, so this was certainly new territory for me.

Finally, Mr. Drake broke the silence and said,
"Donald, come with me: I will take you to the pastor."

"Pastor Ramey, this is Donald Gossett. His dad
owns that poolhall down there on Main Street. His
parents operate the Highway Cafe, that tavern out there

on the highway. Oh, yes, his dad also has that gambling hall down there on South Broadway."

I wanted to scream out in protest, "Please, please, Mr. Drake, don't tell Pastor Ramey who my father is, and what he does for a living! I'm trying to escape that kind of life."

Actually, all the time the deacon was introducing me, my head was dropped in shame. I felt embarrassed and disgraced by what he said. I was not proud of my dad's sinful life. As a matter of fact, I hated it. I had hoped that being identified with an institution like the church would help erase some of the stigma I felt was on my life because I was "Bob Gossett's boy."

The pastor sensed my obvious shame. He put a reassuring hand on my shoulder and looked into my eyes. "Donald, I will present your desire for water baptism and church membership to our church board," he told me. "We will let you know."

I felt it was hopeless. As I drove past that same Baptist church a few days ago, I could visualize in my memory that unforgettable night. In embarrassment and despair I made a beeline for the door and darted with my head down into the night.

That summer night long ago I walked the streets, thinking about the stigma I bore. I fought back tears of discouragement and despair. I felt I was classified as a member of a "bad class" because of my dad's drinking and worldly business activities.

"Oh Lord," I prayed, "I want You in my life. But I just can't belong. I didn't want that pastor to know who my dad is. I wanted to escape that, but it's not possible.

All right, Lord, I am not good enough to belong to a church. So I won't go back any more. I love You, Lord, and I want You to be my Savior. But I just can't go back to that church any more."

I realized later that my thinking was not very mature, but back then I was only 13, and already possessed with so much timidity that it was difficult to cope with life. I walked on through the night, making my way home with one prevailing thought: "Because my name is 'Gossett,' I don't belong to the Christian crowd. I must accept the fact that I am Bob Gossett's boy. I must go on and live with it."

I felt very sad and dejected to realize that, as far as I could determine, I was excluded from Christian fellowship and Christian church services. It was a heartbreaking night for me. I thought that I would never return to church — ever!

Sunday after Sunday came and went, and I didn't go to church, even though my heart ached for the privilege. The weeks stretched into months, the months into years — two long years, actually, before I would ever enter a church again.

When I was 15, a "religious emphasis" week was conducted in our high school. Each morning for one hour, a wonderful Baptist pastor from another city would address the entire student body. I was so hungry to hear his messages that I could hardly wait till the appointed hour. The desire for the gospel and for Jesus Christ was yet uppermost in my thoughts. These services whetted my appetite afresh.

When I heard the pastor announce he was speaking that weekend at the same Baptist church I had left two years previously, I decided I would change my decision and return to church. For my young life, that was a historic decision. I would never be the same again!

To my surprise, I discovered I was actually welcome in that church. Everyone was so kind. I knew I had been missing this beautiful time of Christian worship with other believers. It wasn't long before I was coping with this traumatic experience of my youth by being baptized in water and becoming a member of that fine church. "I can do all things through Christ."

Learning how to cope with my dad's drinking reached a near-fatal climax the summer I turned 16. Once again, it started with one of those drunken orgies that affected our lives so deeply.

That time, my dad was gone from home for a couple of days, accompanied by his brother and two females. Bad news travels fast, and word leaked back to us concerning where Dad was and what he was up to.

My good, moral mother knew she couldn't trust Dad when he was away. Only too well did she know his weakness for the bottle and for other women: it had been her lifelong experience with him. Even so, she was devastated when she learned of his latest escapade.

I can vividly recall the scene when Dad finally returned home in mid-afternoon at the conclusion of his binge. He was anything but sober as he staggered through the door.

"Where have you been?" Mother screamed at him. "Who have you been with? What have you been doing?"

Dad deliberately ignored her. He had only one ambition: he wanted to sleep off his drunk.

Frustrated by Dad's refusal to talk, Mother screamed all the louder. Dad made his way to our front porch and the big swing out there. He stretched out and was asleep almost instantly.

Mother tried to shake him awake, so he would talk with her. But by now he had passed out.

Poor Mother was furious. Dad owed her an explanation of his activities, and all she had on her hands was a passed-out drunk! She became desperate. Deciding that she wouldn't accept his non-communicative response, she quickly went to the refrigerator and got out a pitcher of ice water. Running out to the porch, she flung the ice water over his face with a vengeance.

Needless to say, Dad awakened with a start. He was now wide awake, drunk, and furious.

Shaking the water from his head, Dad charged into the house and ran to his bedroom. There he picked up his favorite .22 rifle, which he always kept loaded. Like a raging bull, he stormed into the next room, where Mom was. He put the rifle on his shoulder, and — with the gun pointed straight at her — he cocked the rifle. He was just about to squeeze the trigger as I rushed into the room to witness this scene of horror.

Dad stood there cursing Mom with every breath. "Now you are done for," he threatened. "I am going to kill you!"

I realized I must act quickly if Mother's life was to be spared. I hit the gun with a sharp blow, causing the rifle to drop to the floor. Both Dad and I scrambled to the floor to retrieve it. Since I was younger and faster — and sober — I yanked the loaded gun from Dad's grasp and handed it to a cousin of mine.

"Run for the woods!" I told him. "Don't come back until I come for you."

Along with everything else, my dad was notorious as a fighter. He was a capable "bouncer" in his tavern and poolhall. It was like a nightmare when I realized my dad was turning on me — to fight me. In a sober condition, Dad never would have fought with his own son. But crazed with "demon drink," he was violently angry — angry enough to shoot my mother, and angry enough to vent his wrath upon me for preventing it.

For a moment, I was tempted to fear. Then I reminded myself, "I can do all things through Christ which strengtheneth me," and turned to face my father. Dad made a couple of wild swings, which I was able to dodge. One of Dad's arms was artificial, made of steel and leather. A single blow from that steel arm had knocked out more than one man!

At 16, I was very strong because of my participation in high-school sports. I had studied wrestling, so I decided to employ a wrestling hold on Dad: it would be my only chance of vanquishing him. I put a hold around his neck and wrestled him to the floor. With all the strength I could muster, I totally subdued my father.

As Dad surrendered to my control, he relaxed. The fiery light went out of his eyes, and things began to calm down in our troubled home. Slowly I let him up, and the two of us stood there eyeing each other.

Dad didn't exactly congratulate me on my achievement, but he did say in a tone of admiration, "You're quite a man, aren't you, son."

Mother and Dad began to talk in a calmer, civilized manner. Both of them were shocked to realize how close they had come to having a fatality take place in our home.

Through it all, I learned that Philippians 4:13, "I can do all things through Christ which strengtheneth me," was more than a motto. It was a promise from God that stood the test in time of need. I knew that as long as I depended on the supernatural Christ who indwelt my life, I would be able to cope with whatever came across my pathway.

I am grateful that two years after this incident, God used me to lead my entire family — including my father — to a saving knowledge of the Lord Jesus Christ. Dad was delivered from his drinking habit! Jesus came into the Gossett home. No longer was Gossett a name that stood for sin and degradation. Jesus Christ had become Lord and Master of the Gossett family!

RX for Action:

No matter what your situation is, there are certain steps you can take that will start to bring about a solution. The most important one is this: get to know the Problem Solver. Then you can say with assurance, "I can do all things through Christ which strengtheneth me" (Philippians 4:13).

Promises of Salvation

People call it "being saved," "being born again," or "becoming a Christian," but no matter what words they use, the Bible teaches us that this experience is necessary before we can become righteous in God's sight — and only the righteous can claim the promises of God with any certainty.

When you become a born-again believer, you become a member of God's family. Before, He was your Creator; afterwards, He is your Father. Unless you have been born again, whether you are aware of it or not, "Ye are of your father the devil" (John 8:44). After you accept Jesus as your Savior, your spirit is re-created and you become a "new creature" (2 Corinthians 5:17), one who is "born of God" (1 John 5:1).

Do you want this experience? It's yours for the asking, as promised by the following Scriptures:

Behold, I stand at the door, and knock: if any man hear my voice, and open the door, I will come in to him, and will sup with him, and he with me.

REVELATION 3:20

But what saith it? The word is nigh thee, even in thy mouth, and in thy heart: that is, the word of faith, which we preach: That if thou shalt confess with thy mouth the Lord Jesus, and shalt believe in thine heart that God hath raised him from the dead, thou shalt be saved. For with

the heart man believeth unto righteousness; and with the mouth confession is made unto salvation.
ROMANS 11:8-10

For whosoever shall call upon the name of the Lord shall be saved.
ROMANS 11:13

Whosoever shall confess that Jesus is the Son of God, God dwelleth in him, and he in God.
1 JOHN 4:15

For he hath made him to be sin for us, who knew no sin; that we might be made the righteousness of God in him.
2 CORINTHIANS 5:21

For God so loved the world, that he gave his only begotten Son, that whosoever believeth in him should not perish, but have everlasting life. For God sent not his Son into the world to condemn the world; but that the world through him might be saved.
JOHN 3:16, 17

Being justified by faith, we have peace with God through our Lord Jesus Christ.
ROMANS 5:1

Chapter Three

How to Cope
With Guilt

Oddly enough, both saints and sinners suffer from a sense of guilt. There is a difference, however, between a SENSE of guilt and REAL guilt. A sense of guilt is a feeling — you FEEL responsible for having done something wrong. Real guilt is a fact — you ARE responsible for having done something wrong.

Guilt feelings can ruin your personality, but true guilt can ruin your destiny — it can send you to hell. This is not God's will for you: God is "not willing that any should perish, but that all should come to repentance" (2 Peter 3:9). Hell wasn't even created for man. Jesus tells us, in Matthew 25:41, that the everlasting fire was "prepared for the devil and his angels." Yet if the Bible teaches anything, it clearly reveals the reality of a place called hell.

According to the Bible, hell is the eternal state of those who die without Christ. Those who refuse to receive Christ as Savior and Lord " ... shall be punished with everlasting destruction from the presence

of the Lord, and from the glory of his power"
(2 Thessalonians 1:9).

True guilt is the fact of having done something
wrong — and the Bible teaches us that having done
something wrong deserves the death penalty.
"The wages of sin" (what you earn by sin) "is death"
(Romans 6:23).

Billy Graham has written, "No matter how
excruciating or how literal the fire of hell may or may not
be, the thirst of a lost soul for the living water will be
more painful than the fires of perdition. Hell, essentially
and basically, is banishment from the presence of God
for deliberately rejecting Jesus Christ as Savior and
Lord. I find no pleasure in the knowledge of the fact of
hell, but I find it my solemn duty to remind you that the
same book that proclaims the wonders of heaven also
describes the terrors of eternal banishment from God."

I agree with Billy Graham that God will never send
anybody to hell. If man goes to hell, he goes by his own
free choice. God never meant that man should go there,
and God has done everything within His power to keep
people out of hell, He even gave His Son to die on the
Cross to keep them out of hell.

When God made you, He made you a free moral
agent. You can live any kind of life you want to. You
can live a good life, or you can live a bad life. You can
break all of God's laws, or you can obey them. You can
go to heaven — or to hell. The choice is yours.

The Bible makes it clear that hell will be a place of
consciousness, completely alone and separated from the
presence of God. The ideas of soul sleep, the crossing of

an icy river, or the hope of a second chance are not
found in the Bible. Second Corinthians 6:2 says,
"Behold, now is the accepted time; behold, now is the
day of salvation."

The idea that there will be some kind of great
fellowship of sinners in hell has no Bible basis either. As
far as we understand God's Word, the sentence is to a
state of torment where a sinner will have to live with his
memories. The knowledge that he could have evaded hell
will plague the sinner throughout eternity.

"What about purgatory?" The purgatory idea has no
basis in Scripture. Nor does the Bible teach complete
annihilation. Rather, it teaches that hell is a place of
never-ending torment for the unsaved.

Speaking of a rich man who went to hell, Jesus said
that "in hell he lifted up his eyes, being in torments, and
seeth Abraham afar off, and Lazarus in his bosom. And
he cried and said, Father Abraham, have mercy on me,
and send Lazarus, that he may dip the tip of his finger in
water, and cool my tongue; for I am tormented in this
flame" (Luke 16:23, 24).

Since true guilt will send us to hell, how can we
possibly cope with it? The good news of the gospel is
that we don't have to cope with guilt — we can get
rid of it.

We saw earlier that the Bible says that the wages of
sin — what we earn by sin — is death. Actually,
according to the Bible, there are two deaths. There is the
death of our body, the "first death," and then there is the
death of our spirit, which the Bible calls "the second
death." Since spirits are eternal — spirits never cease to

exist — "the second death" is being condemned to spend eternity in hell. At the Last Judgment, even our bodies will be resurrected: "they that have done good, unto the resurrection of life; and they that have done evil, unto the resurrection of damnation" (John 5:29).

You've heard people say, "I have good news, and I have bad news." Well, the bad news is that you deserve to die. The good news is that Jesus Christ died in your place. He "took the rap" for you, and if you will allow Him to be your Savior, if you will accept His sacrifice on your behalf, God will erase your name off the list of those sentenced to die and will write it in the Lamb's Book of Life.

"But you don't know what I've done!" someone is thinking. It doesn't matter what you've done: the Word of God declares that there is salvation for all. "For whosoever shall call upon the name of the Lord shall be saved" (Romans 10:13). Salvation is within the reach of every person. There's no need for any to be lost and without God for time and eternity. There's no need for any to die and go to hell. The Bible says, "It is a fearful thing to fall into the hands of the living God" (Hebrews 10:31).

When you accept God's gift of salvation, purchased for you through the blood of Jesus Christ, you are saved from the guilt of your past transgressions. "I, even I, am he that blotteth out thy transgressions for mine own sake, and will not remember thy sins" (Isaiah 43:25). No record is kept of sins forgiven.

Perhaps you have committed sins which you'd like to forget but cannot. God, however, can forget them —

and He does. "There is therefore now no condemnation to them which are in Christ Jesus, who walk not after the flesh, but after the Spirit" (Romans 8:1).

When you receive Christ into your heart you are saved from the power of sin. Sin no longer has dominion over you. The devil's hold is torn loose. Every chain of sin has been broken. Peace, joy and freedom are your heritage in God. You become a new creature in Christ Jesus and are saved from the effects of sin and the wrath to come.

When you accept Jesus, you are saved from the torments of hell where the worm dieth not and the fire is never quenched. Your name is written in the Book of Life. You become a child of the King. A home is being prepared for you in the mansions of Eternity. You are saved to wear crowns of righteousness that will outshine the brightness of the noonday sun and to sing the praises of God forever and ever.

You need not wait. There's salvation for you now. God is offering you the shed blood of His Son as payment for your sins. He's waiting to lift your burden of sin and guilt.

RX for Action:

If you are willing to receive salvation, why not pray right now: *"Heavenly Father, I believe that Jesus died on the Cross, and that you raised Him from the dead. I ask you to forgive my sins, and I now receive Jesus as my Lord and Savior. Amen."*

What to Do After You Say 'Amen'

If you prayed the prayer on the preceding page sincerely, you have just received eternal life. Romans 10:9, 10 says, "That if thou shalt confess with thy mouth the Lord Jesus, and shall believe in thine heart that God hath raised him from the dead, thou shalt be saved. For with the heart man believeth unto righteousness; and with the mouth confession is made unto salvation." Romans10:13 says, "For whosoever shall call upon the name of the Lord shall be saved."

As a newborn Christian, you have new life — God's life — inside of you. Because you are twice-born, you will always be different from the people of this world. God is now your Father, and all of His children throughout the world are now your brothers and sisters.

You wouldn't put a new born infant out on the sidewalk to fend for itself. In the same way, you shouldn't leave your newborn spirit to fend for itself. Here are some of the things that you can do to provide the necessary care and nourishment for the new life within your spirit.

BAPTISM is an outward sign of an inward work of grace. Now that you have been born again, you should be baptized in water according to the command of Jesus. Some people have been baptized as infants, before they were saved. One pastor I know says this: "Baptism is the immersion in water of a saved person. If you weren't saved when you got baptized, you didn't get baptized — you just got wet!" If you are truly serious about your salvation, you will be baptized in water as soon as possible. Jesus said, "He that believeth and is baptized shall be saved; but he that believeth not shall be damned" (Mark 16:16).

BIBLE READING is the food your spirit feeds on. Peter wrote, "As newborn babes, desire the sincere milk of the word, that ye may grow thereby" (1 Peter 2:2).

PRAYER is simply talking to God. When you talk to Him, expect Him to answer you, and when you make requests of Him, expect Him to meet your needs. Jesus said, "Verily, verily, I say unto you, Whatsoever ye shall ask the Father in my name, he will give it you" (John 16:23). You can find God's will revealed in the Bible. "And this is the confidence that we have in him, that, if we ask any thing according to his will, he heareth us: And if we know that he hear us, whatsoever we ask, we know that we have the petitions that we desired of him" (1 John 5:14, 15).

FELLOWSHIP with other Christians is important to your spiritual growth. "And let us consider one another to provoke unto love and to good works: Not forsaking the assembling of ourselves together, as the manner of some is; but exhorting one another ... " (Hebrews 10:24, 25). I would go so far as to say that nobody in the world can live a good Christian life without keeping good company. Bad company ruined Samson and Solomon. It caused Peter to swear and to deny his Lord. Be like the psalmist who said, "I was glad when they said unto me, let us go into the house of the Lord" (Psalm 122:1).

RESIST TEMPTATION. "There hath no temptation taken you but such as is common to man: but God is faithful, who will not suffer you to be tempted above that ye are able; but will with the temptation also make a way to escape, that ye may be able to bear it" (1 Corinthians 10:13). Remember that it is not a sin to be tempted to do wrong; it is a sin only when you yield to that temptation. Trust Jesus to give you daily victory and cleansing through His precious blood. "If we confess our sins, he is faithful and just to forgive us our sins, and to cleanse us from all unrighteousness" (1 John 1:9).

PRAISING THE LORD is one of the greatest secrets of constant spiritual victory. Praise will work wonders in your life. Your life will be a witness to others of God's goodness and will glorify the great and wonderful God whom you love and serve. "Whoso offereth praise glorifieth me ... " (Psalm 50:32).

THE BAPTISM OF THE HOLY SPIRIT is absolutely essential if you want to live in the realm of the miraculous. Be sure to attend a church that believes in the baptism of the Holy Spirit with the evidence of speaking in tongues. Praying in tongues will build up your faith (Jude 20); it will help you pray according to the will of God (Romans 8:26, 27); and it will give you your own special language with which your spirit can communicate with God (1 Corinthians14:2). In addition, you need this enduement of power to possess the ability of God in all activities of your Christian life.

SOULWINNING is the Christian activity closest to Jesus' heart, and as His follower you must be more concerned about winning souls than about anything else you do. Pray daily for the lost; witness and testify to the Lord's saving grace in your own life at every opportunity; give to soul-winning ministries.

TITHES AND OFFERINGS will keep your finances in good shape. (See Malachi 3:8-12 and Luke 6:38). A tithe is 10 percent: God owns the first 10 percent of anything you earn. You owe God the tithe: offerings are love gifts you give to God in addition to your tithes.

Finally, if doubts should come concerning your salvation, rely on the Word of God for your assurance. Remember, God cannot lie; it is the devil who is a liar and a thief. Satan would like to deceive you and steal the blessings of God away from you, but he can do nothing unless you let him. Daily present yourself — spirit, soul, and body — as a vessel of honor for the Lord's service. Tell Him, "Lord, I will go where you want me to go; I will do what you want me to do," and the devil will have to flee. "Submit yourselves therefore to God. Resist the devil, and he will flee from you. Draw nigh to God, and he will draw nigh to you" (James 4:7, 8).

Chapter Four

How to Cope
With Raising Children

Joyce and I are the parents of five children. All five of them are grown now, but many years ago, we adopted the motto: "God gave us kids, not angels."

The Bible teaches that, as parents, we have the responsibility for training and disciplining our children, so that they may be brought up to love the Lord and honor the teachings of the Scriptures.

Child-rearing is so important in God's eyes that the destinies of entire peoples have often hinged upon this one responsibility.

A curse was put upon the house of Eli because, although Eli was a godly man, his two sons were "sons of Belial; they knew not the Lord" (1 Samuel 2:12). Eli knew that his sons would take meat from the offerings before they were offered, and he knew that they would lie with the women of the congregation. We know from the Word that Eli scolded his sons for their sins; yet we also know from the Word that mere words were not enough: God told Eli that he was honoring his sons above the Lord (verse 29), and pronounced a curse upon his family:

> Behold, the days come, that I will cut off thine arm, and the arm of thy father's house, that there shall not be an old man in thine house. And thou shalt see an enemy in my habitation, in all the wealth which God shall give Israel: and there shall not be an old man in thine house for ever. And the man of thine, whom I shall not cut off from mine altar, shall be to consume thine eyes, and to grieve thine heart: and all the increase of thine house shall die in the flower of their age ...

Speaking of Eli, God told Samuel, "For I have told him that I will judge his house for ever for the iniquity which he knoweth; because his sons make themselves vile, and he restrained them not" (1 Samuel 3:13).

Abraham, on the other hand, was blessed by God because God knew that Abraham would raise his children to keep God's ways: "And the LORD said, Shall I hide from Abraham that thing which I do; Seeing that Abraham shall surely become a great and mighty nation, and all the nations of the earth shall be blessed in him? For I know him, that he will command his children and his household after him, and they shall keep the way of the LORD, to do justice and judgment; that the LORD may bring upon Abraham that which he hath spoken of him" (Genesis 18:17-19).

Abraham and Eli were both men of God; yet God judged their lives by how they raised their children.

The Bible makes it very clear that the basic reason for unhappiness in the home is the fact that people disregard the principles that God has given us for child-rearing. People refuse to acknowledge or follow the Lord's plan for the family.

In our study of the Bible, Joyce and I discovered that children in the home are to be taught to obey their parents. Colossians 3:20 says, "Children obey your parents in all things; for this is well pleasing unto the Lord." In Deuteronomy we read that under the Law, "If a man have a stubborn and rebellious son, which will not obey the voice of his father, or the voice of his mother, and that, when they have chastened him, will not hearken unto him ... all the men of his city shall stone him with stones, that he die: so shalt thou put evil away from among you; and all Israel shall hear, and fear" (Deuteronomy 21:18, 21).

Because of the Word of God, Joyce and I never adhered to the popular philosophy which says, "Let your children do as they please." On the other hand, we also knew that as parents, we were not to be unreasonable. Ephesians 6:4 says, "Provoke not your children to wrath: but bring them up in the nurture and admonition of the Lord"; and Colossians 3:21 confirms this when it says, "Fathers, provoke not your children to anger, lest they be discouraged."

Obedience doesn't come naturally to children: they have to be taught to obey their parents, for children are rebellious by nature. In the same way that children have to be taught to read and write, they also have to be taught obedience.

Joyce and I discovered that teaching our children obedience to us at home went a long way towards teaching them obedience to God in later life. It made a positive difference in their willingness to obey the Lord and receive Him as Savior.

What a joy it was for Joyce and me to dedicate each new baby to the Lord, to give him back to the God who had created him. From the time they were very small, Joyce and I would tenderly lay our hands on their little heads and ask God to work His purposes in each life. Then, as now, prayer was the most important ingredient in raising our children to love the Lord.

I must give credit where credit is due. My dear wife, Joyce, was the one who had to cope with most of the problems of raising children. This was because of my calling to be an evangelist, which meant being away from my family a great deal of the time.

The Lord gave my wife real insight concerning how to train children. She learned not to expect more of a child than he was able to do at his age. Joyce always had lists of rules, and she would make it clear to each child what his responsibilities were, and what she expected him to do. Joyce's lists were definite and concise. Of course, we also knew the importance of setting a good example for them, of having prayer in our home each and every day, of taking our children to church and Sunday School, and of teaching them the necessity of taking all their problems to the Lord Himself.

In coping with children, I don't think Joyce and I were harsh about the methods of punishment. We learned to distinguish between willful defiance and childish irresponsibility. We didn't punish the children for things they couldn't help, such as accidentally spilling milk. We always let our children know when they were punished exactly why they were being punished. We let them know that what they had done was wrong, but that we still loved them.

I know it was not easy for our children to take, but I always made it a practice to make a point of forgiving them and giving them a big hug after they had been spanked, and after they had truly repented. Sometimes they were hesitant to embrace after they'd just been spanked, but it always worked wonders. Also, we learned never to bring up their misdeeds again. We let them be forgotten, even as God forgives our sins.

When you must punish your children, be as just and as reasonable as is humanly possible. This means NOT punishing your children simply out of anger and frustration. Remember, too, that your parental responsibility includes your child's behavior at church, at school, and wherever he goes, as well as at home.

The well-known child counselor, Dr. James Dobson, has said that the goal of discipline is to "shape the will without breaking the spirit" (the child's sense of his own self-worth). One thing Joyce would never stand for was for anyone to demean a child's personhood or to say things that were destructive to his self-image; never to call him names.

More than once, Joyce and I made a very important effort to see that our children were properly recognized when we moved to a new community. If we found that they were being put down because of being new in town, we would make it a point to seek out the parents of the culprits, or to go to school and lodge our complaint. We insisted that our children be treated with dignity and respect by everyone. Thank God, this attitude achieved wonders.

When Joyce and I were raising children, the public schools were considerably better than they are today. Conditions vary from city to city and from school to school, but many of the problems that you have in raising children may stem from the things that are happening away from home.

Back in the "good old days," serious discipline offenses in public schools included such things as chewing gum, talking in class, running in the halls, and throwing spitballs. Today, the public schools have to contend with such matters as rape, robbery, drug and alcohol abuse, assault, burglary, unwed mothers, and more.

In a book entitled *Globalism: America's Demise,* William Bowen, Jr. cites several education "authorities" as saying that any child who believes in God and/or country is mentally ill. Perhaps the most extensive of these quotes is on pages 19 and 20, where Bowen quotes an address made by Dr. Pierce of Harvard University, speaking to 2,000 teachers in Denver, Colorado. Dr. Pierce said:

Every child in America who enters school at
the age of five is mentally ill, because he comes
to school with allegiance toward our elected
officials, toward our founding fathers, toward
our institutions, toward the preservation of this
form of government ... patriotism, nationalism,
sovereignty ... All of that proves the children are
sick, because the truly well individual is
one who has rejected all of those things and is
what I would call the true international child of
the future.

In addition, Bowen quotes Paul Brandwein as
saying in his book, *The Social Sciences,* published by
Harcourt Brace that "Any child who believes in God is
mentally ill," and Ashley Montagu as saying in a lecture
to 1,000 teachers at Anaheim, California, that "The
American family structure produces mentally-ill
children." Evidently, "mental illness" is a catch-all label
that humanists now use to stigmatize those who disagree
with their views — and they call *Christians* intolerant!

Christian parents need to be aware that the public
school system is often busily at work trying to undo in
school much of what parents have painstakingly taught at
home. Just a few of the problem areas are as follows:

Mandatory co-ed sex education classes starting as
early as kindergarten promote such practices as
masturbation, fantasizing, diverse lifestyles, and
experimentation with homosexuality and other
perversions. In addition, in some school districts, pupils

are excused from class in order to have abortions without the knowledge of their parents.

"Values clarification" (sometimes taught as a separate subject, and sometimes taught in the course of a more traditional subject) subjects students to the demonic doctrine that there are no moral absolutes, that there is no one independent standard (such as the Word of God) by which actions can be judged.

Meditation, guided imagery, Dungeons and Dragons, and other occult practices take place in many public classrooms.

In science classes, the theory of evolution is taught as a truth; the creation account is regarded as a myth.

Students are taught humanist, rather than biblical beliefs. They are taught the centrality of man, rather than God; that man, rather than God, is the supreme authority; that man is a product of evolution, rather than created by God; that morality is man-made rather than God-made; that salvation is by man's science rather than God's sacrifice. If the parents disagree with what the schools are teaching, students are taught to disregard their parents' "old, outmoded beliefs."

Some Christian parents need to stop blaming themselves for the way their children have turned out and place the blame where it belongs: with the public school system. With things like this happening in the schools, it is no wonder that Christian parents are facing difficult days. More than ever before, many Christian parents are seeking prayer and counseling in order to try to cope with the monsters the public schools have been making of their children.

I have good news for Christian parents: all is not lost. Now, as always, I will repeat that prayer is the most important ingredient in your child's upbringing. Certainly it is important to teach your children God's ways, to have daily family prayer and Bible reading. But just as certainly, it is crucial in times like these to surround your children with prayer and intercession.

Prayer has saved many who were never raised in a Christian home: think how much more effective the intercession of a believing parent will be on a child raised in the ways of God!

Bathe your children in prayer. Believe that God will keep them. Ask God to show you what to permit and what to forbid. Ask Him to show you when you need to intercede. Ask Him for wisdom in fulfilling your parental responsibilities. Maintain scriptural order in your home. Claim the promises of God concerning the salvation of your children. Above all, remember that when you can't cope, God can.

Scriptures that Will Bless Your Family

Here are some promises to claim on your children's behalf:

Train up a child in the way he should go: and when he is old, he will not depart from it.

PROVERBS 2:6

Correct thy son, and he shall give thee rest; yea, he shall give delight unto thy soul.
PROVERBS 29:17

And all thy children shall be taught of the Lord; and great shall be the peace of thy children.
ISAIAH 54:13

As for me, this is my covenant with them, saith the LORD; My spirit that is upon thee, and my words which I have put in thy mouth, shall not depart out of thy mouth, nor out of the mouth of thy seed, nor out of the mouth of thy seed's seed, saith the LORD, from henceforth and for ever.
ISAIAH 59:21

Believe on the Lord Jesus Christ, and thou shalt be saved, and thy house.
ACTS 16:31

Delight thyself also in the LORD; and he shall give thee the desires of thine heart. Commit thy way unto the LORD; trust also in him; and he shall bring it to pass.
PSALM 37:4, 5

And here are some Scriptures every parent needs to take to heart:

And thou shalt love the Lord thy God with all thine heart, and with all thy soul, and with all thy might. And these words, which I command thee this day, shall be in thine heart; and thou shalt teach them diligently unto thy children, and shalt talk of them when thou sittest in thine house, and when thou walkest by the way, and when thou liest down, and when thou risest up.

DEUTERONOMY 6:5-7

He that spareth his rod hateth his son; but he that loveth him chasteneth him betimes.

PROVERBS 13:24

Chasten thy son while there is hope, and let not thy soul spare for his crying.

PROVERBS 19:18

Train up a child in the way he should go, and when he is old, he will not depart from it.

PROVERBS 22:6

Foolishness is bound up in the heart of a child, but the rod of correction shall drive it far from him.

PROVERBS 22:15

And ye fathers, provoke not your children to wrath; but bring them up in the nurture and admonition of the Lord.

EPHESIANS 6:4

That they may teach the young women to be sober, to love their husbands, to love their children.

TITUS 2:4

Chapter Five

How to Cope
With Financial Difficulties

Poverty is not part of God's plan for His people.

It is true that the Bible tells us not to trust in riches: "How hard it is for them that trust in riches to enter the Kingdom of God," Jesus told His followers (Mark 10:24). Money, however, was not the problem Jesus was discussing: He was preaching about priorities. "Where do you put your trust?" Jesus was asking. "Do you trust in money, or do you trust in God?"

Paul told Timothy that "The LOVE of money is the root of all evil" (1 Timothy 6:10, emphasis added). Again, the Bible is speaking about attitude. You do not have to be rich to love money: a poor man can love money just as much as a rich man can.

A Christian's attitude becomes even more important when tested by financial difficulties. What do you do when bills gobble up most of your earnings? During a time of financial crisis, many Christians wonder whether they would be justified in reducing their giving to the Lord.

In thinking about finances, we need to remember that God's plan for His people is as follows: "Beloved, I wish above all things that thou mayest prosper and be in health, even as thy soul prospereth" (3 John 2). Insufficiency and inadequacy are not part of the Christian life, as planned by God.

Instead of austerity, Jesus came to give abundance. He said, "The thief (the devil) cometh not, but for to steal, and to kill, and to destroy: I am come that they might have life, and that they might have it more abundantly" (John 10:10). The abundant life in Christ includes every area: spiritual, emotional, mental, social, and financial. In Jesus, we have total and bountiful provision for all our needs.

Jesus announced, in Luke 4:18, that the Spirit of the Lord had anointed Him to preach the gospel — the good news — to the poor. What was that good news? It was the good news of total deliverance. It was the good news that "My God shall supply all your need according to his riches in glory by Christ Jesus" (Philippians 4:19). It was the good news that "They that seek the Lord shall not want any good thing" (Psalm 34:10).

The Bible abounds with promises that God will "open the windows of heaven," "provide," "replenish," "satisfy," and "prosper" us. God is not a poverty-stricken God, and He doesn't produce poverty-stricken children.

While Jesus came to give us abundance, Satan would like to give us destruction. He comes, the Bible says, "to steal, and to kill, and to destroy." In Malachi 3:11, he is called "the devourer."

Let me tell you about my sure-fire hedge against financial difficulties.

My wife and I once faced a most perilous time. Our daughter, Jeanne, was born with clubfeet. Shortly after that, my wife was afflicted with rheumatic fever that threatened her life. I had to leave the field of evangelism to care for my sick wife and daughter. Because we had no source of income, things looked very dark.

Desperately, I searched the Bible for an answer to our dilemma. There I discovered 2 Corinthians 9:6, 7, "He which soweth sparingly shall reap also sparingly; and he which soweth bountifully shall reap also bountifully. Every man according as he purposeth in his heart, so let him give; not grudgingly, or of necessity: for God loveth a cheerful giver."

I couldn't understand why God would deal with me about money — the one thing I didn't have! Yet the Bible was His living Word. It had saved my soul; I had purposed in my heart that I would live by it. As I dared to accept God's challenge to sow bountifully, I actually gave my way out of poverty. As I gave, people gave back to me, just as Jesus had promised in Luke 6:38, "Give and it shall be given unto you; good measure, pressed down, and shaken together, and running over, shall men give into your bosom. For with the same measure that ye mete withal it shall be measured to you again."

By cutting back on our tithes and offerings in times of financial crisis, we can actually cut ourselves off from the very source of our help out of those difficulties.

A well-known and very important Scripture on the subject of finances is found in Malachi 3:8-11:

> Will a man rob God? Yet ye have robbed me. But ye say, Wherein have we robbed thee? In tithes and offerings. Ye are cursed with a curse; for ye have robbed me, even this whole nation. Bring ye all the tithes into the storehouse, that there may be meat in mine house, and prove me now herewith, saith the LORD of hosts, if I will not open you the windows of heaven, and pour you out a blessing, that there shall not be room enough to receive it. And I will rebuke the devourer for your sakes, and he shall not destroy the fruits of your ground; neither shall your vine cast her fruit before the time in the field, saith the LORD of hosts.

If you have not been tithing, it's no wonder that you have not been prospering: your finances are cursed. On the other hand, as you pay your tithes and give offerings, God promises to "open you the windows of heaven, and pour you out a blessing, that there shall not be room enough to receive it."

God promises that when we honor Him with our substance by giving Him the firstfruits of all our income, our reward will be prosperity. "Honor the Lord with thy substance, and with the firstfruits of all thine increase: So shall thy barns be filled with plenty, and thy presses shall burst out with new wine" (Proverbs 3:9, 10).

In addition to being faithful with your tithes and offerings, there is another principle of God's supply — one I didn't learn about for many years.

For the first years of our early marriage and ministry, Joyce and I struggled with the question of how to solve our financial problems. We were continually frustrated by one financial crisis after another. Although God undertook and our needs were met, we diligently searched the Scriptures and asked God for more answers about money. Surely, we thought, there had to be an easier way!

Then, several years ago, an incident took place which dramatically altered my perception on approaching God about money matters. The Lord ministered a beautiful principle of supply that I believe will encourage you too.

The day it happened, I was hard at work catching up on a backlog of accumulated mail. I leaned back in the big black chair behind my desk, thinking of our recent trip to South America. This missionary trip had been one of the greatest outreaches of our ministry! What a joy it had been to distribute great volumes of literature in the crusade and to share the gospel through nightly radio broadcasts. Thousands of precious souls had accepted the Savior. Jesus' healing power had touched the sick, resulting in wonderful miracles.

Sweet recollections of overseas ministry filled my soul as I turned back to the large desk covered with magazines, office memos and letters written by our friends while Joyce and I were away.

I was dictating the closing lines of a letter to a distraught mother whose only son was in prison when I heard a quiet knock at the door. My personal assistant entered. Her arms were filled with accounting ledgers, file folders, and envelopes.

"Brother Gossett, here are the current statements and bills you asked to see," she told me. "Let me know when you're finished, and I'll pick them up."

As she left the room, I began reviewing the papers she'd placed before me. Everybody wanted money. The radio stations airing our daily broadcasts. The book printers publishing our pamphlets, cards, and other literature. The firms supplying our office machines and typewriters. A missionary couple in Martinique needing money to translate and print our French literature. The utilities company. The phone company. The need for funds seemed never-ending.

I compared the records of the funds we needed with the balance in our bank account. The ends came nowhere near meeting: we were far from able to pay our bills. I asked myself where the money would come from. We weren't squandering any of the sacred dollars that God had entrusted to us through the gifts of our friends. Yet I couldn't see how we were going to pay our bills.

A wave of panic hit me. Clenching my fists in frustration, I cried out to the Lord:

"Oh, God! Please undertake for these financial needs. Lord, we REALLY need Your help."

I raised my clenched fists to the Lord in earnest supplication. The intensity of my prayers accelerated.

The pitch of my voice raised: "Oh God, please give me the money to meet these obligations!"

I must have prayed this way in desperation for some minutes. After a while, the Lord spoke to me: "Take it easy, Don. To receive my blessings, you must relax in me. As long as your hands are closed, I can't put anything in them."

I opened my eyes to examine my tightly clenched hands. Slowly, I opened them. As I did, I felt the tension and desperation fade away. I relaxed, keenly aware of the Lord's presence.

Again the Lord spoke to me. "Did not I say that I would supply all your need? Then just begin to thank me for supplying those needs according to my riches in glory — not your riches."

God showed me that my tight, closed hands were barriers to receiving His riches. The "open palm" attitude showed my trust in His ability to supply all your needs.

The stack of bills remained unchanged, but not my attitude. Now, I approached the Father once more.

"Thank you, Father, for your riches now!"

With total confidence in Philippians 4:19, which says that "my God shall supply all your need according to his riches in glory by Christ Jesus," I repeated these words over and over: "Thank you, Father, for your riches now."

Judging by the speed with which the Lord supplied enough finances to pay that stack of bills, that open palm attitude must have been very pleasing to God! Since then, I have continued to make every day "Palm Sunday" as I praise the Lord for His supply through His riches.

As I do, I find my faith for finances grows by leaps and bounds. You can't affirm "Thank You, Father, for Your riches now," and continue thinking in terms of lack and financial failure. What a precious faith secret!

As Christians, we can be joyful because we are going to receive our needs from God — and we can also be joyful because we know the blessing of giving. The most joyful Christians I have ever known are those who know the joy of giving.

When we support God's work, we can give joyfully in love because God gave in love — He gave His only begotten Son that we might be reconciled to Him.

God is the greatest Giver of all:

"The gift of God is eternal life" (Romans 6:23).

"Thanks be unto God for his unspeakable gift" (2 Corinthians 9:15).

"For by grace are ye saved through faith: and that not of yourselves: it is the gift of God" (Ephesians 2:8).

James 1:5 says that God "giveth to all men liberally, and upbraideth not."

"Every good gift and every perfect gift is from above, and cometh down from the Father of lights ... " (James 1:17).

All of God's gifts come to us through His Son. "He that spared not his own Son, but delivered him up for us all, how shall he not with him also freely give us all things?" (Romans 8:32).

Jesus Christ is a great giver, for He gave himself for us. "For ye know the grace of our Lord Jesus Christ, that, though he was rich, yet for your sakes he became poor, that ye through his poverty might be rich" (2 Corinthians 8:9).

"Grace be to you and peace from God the Father, and from our Lord Jesus Christ, Who gave himself for our sins, that he might deliver us from this present evil world, according to the will of God and our Father (Galatians 1:3, 4). He is "The Son of God, who loved me, and gave himself for me" (Galatians 2:20).

God has honored us by giving us the fruits of His creative hand. "Blessed be the Lord, who daily loadeth us with benefits ... " (Psalm 68:19). The gracious Giver has bestowed unnumbered blessings upon us in love. Therefore we should follow the command of Christ, "Freely ye have received, freely give" (Matthew 10:8).

Don't let money problems quench your joy. You can overcome by giving more to God's work. Don't let Satan trick you into thinking that in times of financial crisis you can't afford to give to God. You can't afford not to.

Remember that God is your Creator and everything you have is made possible by Him. "The earth is the Lord's and the fullness thereof" (I Corinthians 10:26). "The silver is mine, and the gold is mine, saith the Lord of hosts" (Haggai 2:8). In fact, God rightfully claims all creatures. "For every beast of the forest is mine and the cattle upon a thousand hills. I know all the fowls of the mountains: and the wild beasts of the field are mine ... for the world is mine, and the fullness thereof" (Psalm 50:10-12).

Jesus said, "A man can receive nothing, except it be given him from heaven" (John 3:27). If you have the ability to make money in your work, have you considered your Source? "Thus saith the Lord, thy Redeemer, the Holy One of Israel; I am the Lord thy God which teacheth thee to profit, which leadeth thee by the way that thou shouldest go" (Isaiah 48:17). It is God himself who gives you the power to get material things. "But thou shalt remember the Lord thy God: for it is he that giveth thee power to get wealth ... " (Deuteronomy 8:18). "What hast thou that thou didst not receive?" (1 Corinthians 4:7).

The Bible makes it very clear that riches and honor come from the Lord. "Both riches and honor come of thee, and thou reignest over all; and in thine hand is power and might; and in thine hand it is to make great, and to give strength unto all ... for all things come of thee, and of thine own have we given thee" (1 Chronicles 29:12-14). "Every man also to whom God hath given riches and wealth, and to take his portion, and to rejoice in his labor; this is the gift of God" (Ecclesiastes 5:19).

RX for Action:

Pay your tithes, and keep on giving! Make it your motto, "I Live to Give."

Make every day "Palm Sunday" — approach God with praise for His provision. Keep your faith focused on the Solution rather than the situation.

God has promised in Deuteronomy 8:18 to give you power to get wealth, and He has promised in James 1:5 to give you wisdom. Ask God to give you a plan for financial prosperity. He may show you where to look for work, or where to invest your money, or how to improve your job performance. He may give you an invention! He may simply give you favor with your employers, or cause others to give to you. Don't limit God: but when He shows you something, ACT on it.

The Beatitudes of Tithing

Blessed are the tithers,
For they are obeying one of God's fundamental laws.

Blessed are the tithers,
For they are partners with God.

Blessed are the tithers,
For they are helping to extend the kingdom of God.

Blessed are the tithers,
For they are not guilty of robbing God.

Blessed are the tithers,
For the windows of heaven will open
To pour out upon them both spiritual and material
blessings.

Blessed are the tithers,
For they are the ones who become cheerful givers,
Beloved of God.

The Tither Believes:

1. That God is the owner of all things and man is charged with the responsibility of management for God.

2. That he lives under an obligation each day to seek the kingdom of God and His righteousness.

3. That he has a right to depend upon the love of God under every condition.

4. That there is a sanctity about all possessions since they are the property of God.

5. That God honors the tithe when it is dedicated to Him in a spirit of humility.

6. That tithing establishes a covenant between him and God. It is a mutually profitable and gratifying agreement between God and man. They become partners in the greatest of all life's busy transactions.

When You Tithe, You Will Be Surprised

1. At the amount of money you have for the Lord's work.

2. At the ease with which you are able to meet your own obligations with the remaining nine-tenths.

3. At the deepening of your own spiritual life as you, in obedience, pay your tithes.

4. At the prudent disposal afforded to a faithful and wise steward over the nine-tenths that remain.

5. At the ease with which you will be able to go from giving one-tenth to giving more.

6. At yourself for not becoming a tither sooner.

The Promises of God Include Prosperity

Many Christians resign themselves to a life of poverty because they think it's somehow more "spiritual" to be poor. Actually, however, Proverbs 10:15 points out that "the destruction of the poor is their poverty." Poverty is not God's will for you: His will is revealed in Psalm 107:19, 20, "Then they cry unto the LORD in their trouble, and he saveth them out of their distresses. He sent his word, and healed them. AND DELIVERED THEM FROM THEIR DESTRUCTION."

Once you start looking for them, you can find any number of Scriptures on the subject of prosperity. The following are just a few to get you started. Stand on these Scriptures, be faithful in your tithes and offerings, be obedient to the Word of God, and watch your finances multiply!

Keep therefore the words of this covenant, and do them, that ye may prosper in all that ye do.

DEUTERONOMY 29:9

This book of the law shall not depart out of thy mouth; but thou shalt meditate therein day and night, that thou mayest observe to do according to all that is written therein: for then thou shalt make thy way prosperous, and then thou shalt have good success.

JOSHUA 1:8

And keep the charge of the LORD thy God, to walk in his ways, to keep his statutes, and his commandments, and his judgments, and his testimonies, as it is written in the law of Moses, that thou mayest prosper in all that thou doest, and whithersoever thou turnest thyself.

1 KINGS 2:3

Be ye strong therefore, and let not your hands be weak: for your work shall be rewarded.

2 CHRONICLES 15:7

Blessed is the man that walketh not in the counsel of the ungodly, nor standeth in the way of sinners, nor sitteth in the seat of the scornful. But his delight is in the law of the LORD; and in his law doth he meditate day and night. And he shall be like a tree planted by the rivers of water, that bringeth forth his fruit in his season; his leaf also shall not wither; and whatsoever he doeth shall prosper.

PSALM 1:1-3

The young lions do lack and suffer hunger: but they that seek the LORD shall not want any good thing.

PSALM 34:10

Let them shout for joy, and be glad, that favour my righteous cause: yea, let them say continually, Let the LORD be magnified, which hath pleasure in the prosperity of his servant.

PSALM 35:27

I have been young, and now am old; yet have I not seen the righteous forsaken, nor his seed begging bread.
PSALM 37:25

For the LORD God is a sun and shield: the LORD will give grace and glory: no good thing will he withhold from them that walk uprightly.
PSALM 84:11

Pray for the peace of Jerusalem: they shall prosper that love thee. Peace be within thy walls, and prosperity within thy palaces.
PSALM 122:6, 7

I lead in the way of righteousness, in the midst of the paths of judgment: That I may cause those that love me to inherit substance; and I will fill their treasures.
PROVERBS 8:20, 21

A good man leaveth an inheritance to his children's children: and the wealth of the sinner is laid up for the just.
PROVERBS 13:22

He that covereth his sins shall not prosper: but whoso confesseth and forsaketh them shall have mercy.
PROVERBS 28:13

Cast thy bread upon the waters: for thou shalt find it after many days.
ECCLESIASTES 11:1

If ye be willing and obedient, ye shall eat the good of the land.

ISAIAH 1:19

Say ye to the righteous that it shall be well with him: for they shall eat the fruit of their doings.

ISAIAH 3:10

Thus saith the LORD, thy Redeemer, the Holy One of Israel; I am the LORD thy God which teacheth thee profit, which leadeth thee by the way that thou shouldest go.

ISAIAH 48:17

But seek ye first the kingdom of God and his righteousness; and all these things shall be added unto you.

MATTHEW 6:33

Give, and it shall be given unto you; good measure, pressed down, and shaken together, and running over, shall men give into your bosom. For with the same measure that ye mete withall it shall be measured to you again.

LUKE 6:38

And God is able to make all grace abound toward you; that ye, always having all sufficiency in all things, may abound to every good work.

2 CORINTHIANS 9:8

But my God shall supply all your need according to his riches in glory by Christ Jesus.

PHILIPPIANS 4:19

Chapter Six

How to Cope With Poverty

As we have already mentioned, the Bible clearly teaches that God's will for us is prosperity: "Beloved, I wish above all things that thou mayest prosper and be in health, even as thy soul prospereth" (3 John 2). In order that we may prosper, God has outlined a number of poverty-producing situations in His Word, and told us what steps to take in order to avoid poverty and obtain prosperity.

Because it is so clearly God's desire that we prosper, many Christians are taken aback when He also requires us to "maintain an attitude of gratitude" even in the midst of poverty. Paul said, "I have learned, in whatsoever state I am, therewith to be content" (Philippians 4:11), and James commands us to do likewise: "Let the brother of low degree rejoice in that he is exalted: But the rich, in that he is made low: because as the flower of the grass he shall pass away" (James 1:9, 10).

Even in the midst of poverty, God's Word to us is: "Rejoice in the Lord alway: and again I say, Rejoice"

(Philippians 4:5). Rejoice that you have a loving, heavenly Father who has promised to supply your needs. Rejoice that you can cast your cares on Him. Rejoice that you can expect supernatural help, whatever your situation is.

Too often, Christians allow themselves to get down in the dumps over their finances. Discouragement only leads to a state of lethargy in which you won't feel like taking the necessary steps to remedy your situation. So rejoice! No matter what the problem is, God has the answer.

Sometimes poverty is caused by illness. If this is your situation, turn to Chapter 11, "How to Cope with Sickness."

Sometimes poverty is a curse brought on by failure to tithe. (Tithing is giving one-tenth of your increase — your profits or your salary — to God.) If this is your problem, the answer is simple — just start tithing.

Sometimes poverty comes from "living by faith" when God hasn't called you to do so. If you haven't heard the expression "living by faith" before, you may wonder what I'm talking about, since according to Romans 1:17, all Christians are called to live by faith: "As it is written, The just shall live by faith." Many Christians, however use this phrase to refer to having no regular source of income other than that which God provides supernaturally.

It is quite true that God *has* called many in full-time Christian work to "live by faith," and He is quite able to meet their needs. Problems arise, however, when people expect God to give them full-time pay for part-time work: or when they expect God to pay them for a job He hasn't asked them to do. (Would YOU pay a salary to someone you hadn't hired?)

If you are "living by faith" and your needs aren't being met, take the following steps:

(1) Examine your call. Did God ask you to go full-time into the ministry? Did He tell you not to work at a secular job? Did He tell you not to accept a salary?

(2) Examine your faith. Are you BELIEVING that God will meet your needs?

(3) Examine your diligence. Are you expecting God to give you full-time pay for part-time work? Are you just sitting around, waiting for work to come to you, or are you taking steps in the natural to see that doors will open? When doors don't open, are you redeeming the time in Bible study, prayer, and witnessing? Or do you need to check out the following problem area, because ...

Sometimes poverty is caused by laziness.

God forbids anything less than fervency and wholeheartedness in our pursuits. We are to avoid slothfulness and idleness in our work and business. "Not slothful in business; fervent in spirit, serving the Lord" (Romans 12:11).

If you are out of work, make it your business to look for work. Make a full-time job of it. "For even when we were with you, this we commanded you, that if any would not work, neither should he eat. For we hear that there are some which walk among you disorderly, working not at all, but are busybodies. Now them that are such we command and exhort by our Lord Jesus

Christ, that with quietness they work, and eat their own bread" (2 Thessalonians 3:10-12).

Diligence is commanded — and commended — many times throughout the Bible, in both the Old and New Testaments. Ephesians 4:28 says, "Let him that stole steal no more: but rather let him labour, working with his hands the thing which is good, that he may have to give to him that needeth"; 1 Timothy 5:8 reveals that "If any provide not for his own, and specially for those of his own house, he hath denied the faith, and is worse than an infidel"; and 1 Thessalonians 4:11,12 advises "Study to be quiet, and to do your own business, and to work with your own hands, as we commanded you; That ye may walk honestly toward them that are without, and that ye may have lack of nothing."

Are you believing God for something? We are commanded to be diligent not only in our works, but in our faith. Hebrews 6:12 insists "That ye be not slothful, but followers of them who through faith and patience inherit the promises."

Slothfulness produces laziness and apathy. "The slothful man roasteth not that which he took in hunting: but the substance of a diligent man is precious" (Proverbs 12:27). "He also that is slothful in his work is brother to him that is a great waster" (Proverbs 18:9).

Slothfulness leads to poverty. "He becometh poor that dealeth with a slack hand; but the hand of the diligent maketh rich" (Proverbs 10:4). "Love not sleep, lest thou come to poverty: open thine eyes, and thou shalt be satisfied with bread" (Proverbs 20:13).

Lazy people often make excuses for themselves, but the Bible teaches us to overcome obstacles, rather than letting those obstacles overcome us. "The sluggard will not plow by reason of the cold; therefore shall he beg in harvest, and have nothing" (Proverbs 20:4).

Slothfulness is a sin of omission, not a sin of commission. Because it consists of something you're NOT doing, its results sneak up on you. But God tells us to observe the results of slothfulness, to take heed to avoid its downfall: "I went by the field of the slothful, and by the vineyard of the man void of understanding; And, lo, it was all grown over with thorns, and nettles had covered the face thereof, and the stone wall thereof was broken down. Then I saw, and considered it well: I looked upon it, and received instruction" (Proverbs 24:30-32).

Although I warn against the dangers of "living by faith" when you're actually living by presumption, there are some who are called by God to do full-time work without receiving a salary. We've already discussed the fact that some ministers are called to live this way; I would also include most housewives. As any housewife will tell you, caring for a house and children is a full-time job! Although there are some, in this day and age, who do not appreciate a housewife's role, God understands the importance of that calling.

The Lord has given each of us certain talents or gifts, and He expects us to increase these gifts and multiply their effectiveness. "But he that had received one (talent) went and digged in the earth, and hid his lord's money ... His lord answered and said unto him, Thou wicked and slothful servant" (Matthew 25:18,26).

The Lord calls us to be diligent watchmen for Him. He warns us of the folly of being otherwise. "His watchmen are blind: they are all ignorant, they are all dumb dogs, they cannot bark; sleeping, lying down, loving to slumber" (Isaiah 56:10).

Idleness and slothfulness are the marks of a spiritual sluggard. The Lord wants to see the spiritual qualities of fervency of spirit, persistence and wholeheartedness in our lives. We are to avoid idleness and slothfulness in spiritual matters as well as in work and business. "By much slothfulness the building decayeth; and through idleness of hands the house droppeth through" (Ecclesiastes 10:18).

"Whatsoever thy hand findeth to do, do it with thy might," Solomon wrote in Ecclesiastes 9:10. If you are in good health and your life lines up with the Word of God, hard work and persistence are sure to produce prosperity. Here is what Dr. E.W. Kenyon wrote about these important qualities:

> "How did you ever do it? I can't see how any one could do a thing like that?"
>
> We were in a curio shop. On the table there was a whole army of little figures that had been whittled out by hand. What hours must have been spent on them.
>
> This friend of mine stood there, and looking at them said, "How did you ever do it?"
>
> The man smiled, "I just kept at it."

I walked the street and I heard those three words, "Kept at it; kept at it; kept at it."

How they rang through my soul. That man had "kept at it." He had put life into it. He had made a success.

People were coming from all parts of the country to see the effects of that cultivated, trained genius.

All that man had done was to train his mind and hand, and then whittle his dreams out of wood, of soft stone and ivory.

I was thrilled through and through at the possibilities that were wrapped up in common folks like you and me.

I heard a girl play the piano. She was not over 16. I know something about music. We had a music department in our institution for many years.

I looked at her face and I whispered in my own heart, "Girl, you have spent hours pounding the keys while other girls were walking the street. While others were sleeping and mother was trying to get them out of bed, you were pounding those keys.

"You have lost a heap of good times, but what a musician you are!"

She kept at it. That is why she won.

I stood with a man, overlooking a beautiful farm in northern Maine. I said to him, "Who cleared this land? Who stumped it?"

He answered, "Do you see that little log house down there by the creek?

"I built that, and my wife and I moved into it before there was an acre of this land cleared. I vowed that I would clear away every acre on it and put it into crops, and I have done it."

That is the spirit that conquers. "I vowed I would do it, and I have done it."

I stood in the factory as a boy and vowed that I would become an educator. I did not know what it meant, but I knew that within me was a teaching gift, an undeveloped thing.

I vowed that I would do it. I did it. I was handicapped as few men have been handicapped, but I did it.

I am passing it on to you to show that they cannot conquer you if you will to do it.

Struggle to improve. In every effort improve the dream.

Every time you play that piece on the piano, play it better than you played it before.

Every time you sit down to that typewriter, make up your mind that you are going to be more efficient than you have ever been.

Make your brain work. It will sweat, but make it work. It will improve. It will develop until you become a wonder to those around you.

Don't depend on an alarm clock. Don't depend on mother's waking you. Make up your mind that you will have the alarm clock in your soul.

Never depend on another man's car. Get one of your own. Be self-reliant. Be punctual. Be diligent. Think through on every problem. Conquer your difficulties as a part of the day's job. We are out in the fight, and we will win the crown.

I first read these words of Dr. Kenyon's when I was 23. I studied these principles of persistence over and over. I knew by God's grace and hard work I could achieve in those areas to which God had called me.

Two years before, at age 21, the Lord had given me a definite call to radio ministry. I signed a contract with a station and launched my own radio ministry. But, there was never quite enough money to stay on the air so I cancelled the broadcasts.

However, I was persuaded that God had called me. I was not to be denied. Years went by. I would go on the radio for a few months, then off, when the "going got tough." I wrestled with the ability to pay for airtime.

Then in September, 1961, more than 10 years had passed since God had called me to radio ministry. I knew it was time to "take heed to the ministry which I had received of the Lord, that I fulfill it (see Colossians 4:17).

I signed a contract with KARI Radio Station at Birch Bay, Washington. In my heart I was prepared to "keep at it" and succeed in the radio ministry.

Nine listeners wrote to me as a result of my very first broadcast on KARI. That was the beginning of a very fruitful minstry, and I have never looked back!

At first I was on KARI only once a day, at 11 a.m. Then Mr. Don Bevilacqua, the manager, took a vacation up into the northern regions of British Columbia, into the Yukon, the Northwest Territories, and northern Alberta. He discovered that KARI could be heard only in the middle of the night up north.

He talked with me, "Don, some radio preacher ought to be ministering to the night people, especially those who live long distances away. Only in the middle of the night can we be away up in the northern regions of the continent."

I accepted that challenge, and in 1964 I began broadcasting every night of the year at 2 a.m. For more than 20 years, I have never missed a night on the air at 2 a.m.

"Let us not be weary in well doing, for in due season we shall reap, if we faint not" (Galatians 6:10).

In my case, the fulfillment of my radio ministry didn't happen overnight. I prayed and persisted. I tried and failed. I went on the air on stations with zeal, only to retreat months later when funds were not forthcoming to pay the bills. But God helped me to develop patience and determination. I would not be denied.

Whatever you are seeking from the Lord, I encourage you to "keep at it."

If you need healing for your body, establish a foundation upon God's Word whereby you know His promises to heal you. Then keep at it as you exercise your faith, speak the Word, resist the devil, and praise the Lord.

In my acquaintance with many people who have experienced divine healing, this attitude of persistence in faith is highly significant.

"Without faith it is impossible to please him, for he that cometh to God must believe that he is, and that he is a rewarder of them that DILIGENTLY seek him" (Hebrews 11:6, emphasis added).

Keep on reaching out for your miracle — God is a rewarder of them that DILIGENTLY seek Him.

When I was seeking healing for the ugly growth that appeared on my head in 1976, my wife Joyce, and I were persistent in speaking God's Word.

We made a decision that we would speak the Word instead of the problem.

I recalled that a woman in Portland, Oregon, had said to me, "Brother Gossett, all I know the Bible says about healing is about Job's boils, Timothy's sore stomach, and Paul's thorn in the flesh."

I replied, "Lady, there is a whole lot more than that!"

Joyce and I "kept at it" as we believed and confessed God's healing Word. We would say, "The Lord is blessing our bread and our water, and He is taking sickness and its effects off my body." We were paraphrasing Exodus 23:25 and making it personal.

In spite of the fact that the growth was getting larger day by day, we persisted in declaring that "Himself took our infirmities, and bare our sicknesses," according to Matthew 8:17 and Isaiah 53:4.

God helped us to hold fast our confession without wavering, "for he is faithful that promised" (Hebrews 10:23).

After days and weeks of "keeping at it" with God's Word prevailing, that ugly growth had to submit to the authority of the Word. When I was flying home on March 1, 1976, I reached up and touched that growth. One-half of it came off my head!

We maintained our persistent affirmation of God's Word. On the early morning of March 3, I awakened. I reached out to touch my head, and there was nothing there — my head was there, of course, but the growth wasn't!

God had rewarded our faith. He had watched over His Word to perform it. The growth, which had been scheduled for surgery, was miraculously healed. Thousands have heard this testimony of God's miracle power in response to undenying faith.

When I began radio ministry in 1961, the Holy Spirit gave me a plan for sharing my radio messages in printed form. I couldn't afford to publish books, so I developed a card system. On each of these cards, I wrote and printed a message highlighting my messages over the air. First, there was "My Never Again List." It was quite a success. But I visualized hundreds of cards like that one, cards that would share a practical, condensed message with the body of Christ.

I made a list of 40 different titles I would write. I then announced these 40 subjects on a card and invited friends to request them.

I remember how a minister friend laughed at me. He said, "Don, you will never print all those forty cards!"

But that spirit of "keep at it" possessed me. I vowed that I would do it and thank God, I did it. But I didn't stop with those initial 40 Bold Living Cards. I persisted until there were 100 Bold Living Cards. Through these years, God had enabled us to publish multiplied millions of these cards in various languages.

Later, I wrote 100 Confidence Cards. And as of this writing, I'm well on the way to completing 100 Praise Cards, as well as working on 100 Faith Cards.

Do you have unsaved loved ones you desire to win to Christ? Then "keep at it" until God uses you to win those dear ones to our Savior. You can do it. But it will take wholeheartedness and persistence in faith and action.

As you know, I was born and raised in a non-Christian home. Personally, I received Jesus as my Savior and Lord at the age of 12. While I was passive in my faith about my family's salvation, I never got down to business about winning them to the Lord. When I was 18, I became vividly conscious of their lostness, of what the consequences would be if they died in their sins.

One afternoon, I met God in fervent prayer in a pasture. He gave me assurance that if I would persist in my outreach towards my family, I would soon see them all saved. Thank God, that "keep at it" spirit was productive. Within a few months, all of my immediate family was born again, as one by one they came to receive Christ.

God will give you soul-winner's wisdom to know how to influence your loved ones for the Lord. Be active in your faith, instead of passive. Keep at it until they are all in the fold of the Father.

RX for Action:

Keep up your morale by maintaining an attitude of gratitude.

Diagnose your problem: ask God to show you if there is something you are doing that is causing your financial difficulties. Perhaps He'll show you something in the natural realm. It may be the way you handle the money you do have that causes your problems. Or perhaps He'll show you something in the spiritual realm, such as failing to tithe, that is causing you not to prosper.

Be diligent: determine that you are going to "keep at it," no matter what. "In the morning sow seed, and in the evening withhold not thine hand: for thou knowest not whether shall prosper, either this or that, or whether they both shall be alike good" (Ecclesiastes 11:6). Realize that God expects us to be diligent in whatever we do, whether in our secular employment or in our work for Him.

God Promises to Bless the Diligent

You may have had such bad work experiences that you wonder what's the use of even trying. But your employer (or prospective employer) is not the source of your prosperity — God is. And God promises that "whatsoever good thing any man doeth, the same shall he receive of the Lord" (Ephesians 6:8).

Here are some Scriptures on diligence that will encourage you:

The hand of the diligent shall bear rule: but the slothful shall be under tribute.

PROVERBS 12:24

In all labour there is profit.

PROVERBS 14:23

The thoughts of the diligent tend only to plenteousness; but of every one that is hasty only to want.

PROVERBS 21:5

Seest thou a man diligent in his business? He shall stand before kings; he shall not stand before mean men.

PROVERBS 22:29

He that tilleth his land shall have plenty of bread.

PROVERBS 28:19

A good man leaveth an inheritance to his children's children: and the wealth of the sinner is laid up for the just.

PROVERBS 13:32

Let him that stole steal no more: but rather let him labour, working with his hands the thing which is good, that he may have to give to him that needeth.

EPHESIANS 4:28

Chapter Seven

How to Cope
With a Sectarian Spirit

Perhaps one of the greatest thieves of spiritual blessing and power is a spirit of sectarianism — thinking that our own particular group is the only one that is right, or that our own particular denomination has a corner on the market of God's blessings.

The disciples were deceived in this manner. One time they came to Jesus saying, "Master, we saw one casting out devils in thy name; and we forbade him, because he followeth not with us" (Luke 9:49). However, Jesus rebuked these disciples and said, "Forbid him not: for he that is not against us is for us" (verse 50).

Sectarianism divides the body of Christ, arraying Christians one against another. The law of Christ is not sectarianism but unity. The life of Christ is love — not antagonism and animosity toward one another. The badge of true discipleship is that we have love one for another. "By this shall all men know that ye are my disciples, if ye have love one to another" (John 13:35).

Paul ran into a sectarian spirit in the church at Corinth. Here is what he had to say about the problem in 1 Corinthians 3:1-9:

> And I brethren, could not speak unto you as unto spiritual, but as unto carnal, even as unto babes in Christ. I have fed you with milk, and not with meat: for hitherto ye were not able to bear it, neither yet now are ye able. For ye are yet carnal: for whereas there is among you envying, and strife, and divisions, are ye not carnal, and walk as men? For while one saith, I am of Paul; and another, I am of Apollos; are ye not carnal? Who then is Paul, and who is Apollos, but ministers by whom ye believed, even as the Lord gave to every man? I have planted, Apollos watered; but God gave the increase. So then neither is he that planteth any thing, neither he that watereth; but God that giveth the increase. Now he that planteth and he that watereth are one: and every man shall receive his own reward according to his own labour. For we are labourers together with God ...

The Corinthians were a church that some people might think fairly advanced in spiritual things. After all, Paul wrote to them that "ye come behind in no gift" (1 Corinthians 1:7). According to 1 Corinthians 1:5, they had all the utterance gifts and all the revelation gifts flowing freely in their church. They were very charismatic! Paul, however, didn't think the Corinthians were very mature. "I've fed you with milk instead of meat because you're just a bunch of babies," he told them. "I know you're carnal because you still have envying, and strife, and divisions among you — you follow me, or you follow Apollos, instead of realizing that we are all one in Christ!"

If you ever want to grow beyond the "milk" stage in things of God, you are going to have to rid yourself of any hint of sectarianism. Sectarianism is just another form of what the Bible calls "respect of persons," and what James has to say about respect of persons is this: "My brethren, have not faith of our Lord Jesus Christ, the Lord of glory, with respect of person ... If ye fulfill the royal law according to the scripture, Thou shalt love thy neighbour as thyself, ye do well: But if ye have respect to persons, ye commit sin, and are convinced of the law as transgressors" (James 2:1, 8, 9).

Later on in his epistle, James writes, "Who is a wise man and endued with knowledge among you? let him shew out of a good conversation his works with meekness of wisdom. But if ye have bitter envying and strife in your hearts, glory not, and lie not against the truth. This wisdom descendeth not from above, but is earthly, sensual, devilish. For where envying and strife is, there is confusion and every evil work" (James 3:13-16).

Where envy and strife is, James says, there is EVERY EVIL WORK! No wonder Paul couldn't go beyond the basics with the Corinthians — they weren't ready for it. They had envy. They had strife. They had divisions. And we learn in Chapter Six that they also had immorality. Evidently they really did have "every evil work."

The world fights and competes and hates one another because the people of the world are struggling for what they perceive as "their share" of a limited supply of resources. As Christians, however, we serve an unlimited God of unlimited resources.

When Elijah was sent to the widow of Zarephath, he asked her for a morsel of bread. "As the LORD thy God liveth," she told him, "I have not a cake, but an handful of meal in a barrel, and a little oil in a cruse: and, behold, I am gathering two sticks, that I may go in and dress it for me and my son, that we may eat it, and die" (1 Kings 17:12).

"Fear not," Elijah told her, "go and do as thou hast said: but make me thereof a little cake first, and bring it unto me, and after make for thee and for they son. For thus saith the LORD God of Israel, The barrel of meal shall not waste, neither shall the cruse of oil fail, until the day that the LORD sendeth rain upon the earth" (1 Kings 17:13,14). God is able to provide enough for everyone!

If the church down the block grows, we don't have to worry that it will stunt our church's growth: if we will pray for revival, God is more than able to send enough converts to fill BOTH churches!

When Christian TV programs first came on the scene, there were many dire predictions about the negative effects that "the electronic church" would have on local churches. Actually, according to a recent survey conducted by The Gallup Organization, viewers of

Christian television are NO LESS LIKELY to attend or contribute to a local church.

In addition to fear of somehow "losing out" on God's blessings, there is another cause of sectarianism. It, too, is something God detests: self-righteousness. The Bible records in Luke 18:9-14 that Jesus "spake this parable unto certain which trusted in themselves that they were righteous, and despised others."

"Two men went up into the temple to pray," Jesus said, "the one a Pharisee, and the other a publican. The Pharisee stood and prayed thus with himself, God, I thank thee, that I am not as other men are, extortioners, unjust, adulterers, or even as this publican. I fast twice in the week, I give tithes of all that I possess.

"And the publican, standing afar off, would not lift up so much as his eyes unto heaven, but smote upon his breast, saying, God be merciful to me a sinner.

"I tell you, this man went down to his house justified rather than the other: for every one that exalteth himself shall be abased; and he that humbleth himself shall be exalted."

A sectarian spirit is not a mark of maturity — it is a mark of immaturity. It is not a sign that you are "special" in God's kingdom; it is a sign that your spiritual well-being is in dire need of repairs.

RX for Action:

Obey Matthew 19:19, "Thou shalt love thy neighbour as thyself."

Love One Another

The entire gospel is based on love. In God's Word, love is not an option, it's a commandment. Yet how easy it is to fall short of the true gospel standard of love. Here are a few Scriptures that the entire Church needs to live by:

But whoso hath this world's good, and seeth his brother have need, and shutteth up his bowels of compassion for him, how dwelleth the love of God in him? My little children, let us not love in word, neither in tongue; but in deed and in truth.

1 JOHN 3: 17, 18

If a man say, I love God, and hateth his brother, he is a liar: for he that loveth not his brother whom he hath seen, how can he love God whom he hath not seen? And this commandment have we from him, That he who loveth God love his brother also.

1 JOHN 4:20, 21

Whosoever believeth that Jesus is the Christ is born of God: and every one that loveth him that begat loveth him also that is begotten of him.

1 JOHN 5:1

This is my commandment, That ye love one another, as I have loved you. Greater love hath no man than this, that a man lay down his life for his friends.

JOHN 15:12, 13

Above all these things put on charity, which is the
bond of perfectness.

COLOSSIANS 3:14

And let us consider one another to provoke unto
love and to good works.

HEBREWS 10:24

If ye fulfil the royal law according to the scripture,
Thou shalt love thy neighbour as thyself, ye do well.

JAMES 2:8

Seeing ye have purified your souls in obeying the
truth through the Spirit unto unfeigned love of the
brethren, see that ye love one another with a pure heart
fervently.

1 PETER 1:22

Have fervent charity among yourselves: for charity
shall cover the multitude of sins.

1 PETER 4:8

Chapter Eight

How to Cope With the Devil's Devices:
Depression, Insomnia, Stress, Indecision

How do you tell what comes from the devil, and what comes from God?

If you are a born-again Christian, living right and doing right, John 10:10 is an accurate guide to the sources of the things that happen in your life: "The thief cometh not, but for to steal, and to kill, and to destroy: I am come," Jesus said, "that they might have life, and that they might have it more abundantly."

The things that make for an abundant life all come from God. "Every good gift and every perfect gift is from above, and cometh down from the Father of lights, with whom is no variableness, neither shadow of turning" (James 1:17).

Things that steal, things that kill, things that destroy — all these come from Satan. However, as Paul pointed out, "we are not ignorant of his devices" (2 Corinthians 2:11). Not only that, but the Word promises us that we need have no fear of anything the devil can do to us, for we have authority over him. Jesus said, "Behold, I give unto you power to tread on serpents and scorpions, and over ALL the power of the enemy: and nothing shall by any means hurt you" (Luke 10:19). This is why we are told, "Submit yourselves therefore to God. Resist the devil, and he will flee from you" (James 4:7).

In this chapter, I want to talk about four of the devil's many devices, things he brings against Christians to drain their energy and destroy their effectiveness, not only in their work for the gospel, but even in their daily lives. Depression, insomnia, stress and indecision are common problems, but any one of them can rob you of your joy, strength, and vitality. As Christians, we don't need to put up with that! We are not ignorant of the devil's devices, so let's learn to resist him and put him on the run.

How to Cope With Depression

There are various degrees of depression, ranging from a mild case of the "blues" to serious cases requiring psychiatric treatment. Anyone who has ever suffered from depression can testify to its destructive force.

In order to cope with something, you must first recognize its source. Satan is the author of depression. It is one of his favorite tools for ravaging the minds of men and women today.

Evil spirits like depression attempt to oppress you in order to break and crush your spirit. They harass your mind with fear, doubt, and uncertainty. They are the cause of frustration and can destroy your health, your peace of mind, and even the harmony of your home if you do not take dominion over them.

We have already seen that the Bible commands us to "Resist the devil, and he will flee from you" (James 4:7). Refuse to be Satan's dumping ground for mental unsoundness, nervous disorders, or spirits of gloom, heaviness, and depression. Instead, study Matthew 4:1-11, to see how Jesus used the Word of God against the devil. You can do the same thing.

In coping with depression, or anything else that comes from the devil, boldly quote the Word of God against Satan, just as Jesus did. The Word is a Christian's most effective weapon against the enemy. "For the weapons of our warfare are not carnal, but mighty through God to the pulling down of strong holds" (2 Corinthians 10:4).

Know your rights. You are an overcomer. You can defeat all of Satan's works: "And they overcame him (Satan) by the blood of the Lamb, and by the word of their testimony" (Revelation 12:11).

As Christians, we are in a very real warfare with the forces of evil. Ephesians 6:10-18 tells us what our weapons are:

> Finally, my brethren, be strong in the Lord, and in the power of his might. Put on the whole armor of God, that ye may be able to stand against the wiles of the devil. For we wrestle not against flesh and blood, but against principalities, against powers, against the rulers of the darkness of this world, against spiritual wickedness in high places. Wherefore take unto you the whole armor of

God, that ye may be able to withstand in the
evil day, and having done all, to stand. Stand
therefore, having your loins girt about with
truth, and having on the breastplate of
righteousness; And your feet shod with the
preparation of the gospel of peace; Above all,
taking the shield of faith, wherewith ye shall
be able to quench all the fiery darts of the
wicked. And take the helmet of salvation, and
the sword of the Spirit, which is the word of
God: Praying always with all prayer and
supplication in the Spirit, and watching
thereunto with all perseverance and
supplication for all saints ...

Jesus Christ has given you power and authority
over all the power of the devil: "And these signs shall
follow them that believe; In my name shall they cast out
devils" (Mark 16:17). The name of Jesus belongs to you:
dare to use it! Plead the power that's in that name.

Stand your ground fearlessly. Evil spirits of
depression know they must submit to that "name which
is above every name: That at the name of Jesus every
knee should bow, of things in heaven, and things in
earth, and things under the earth" (Philippians 2:9, 10).

Claim the power of God's anointing to disperse
Satan's spirit of gloom. "The yoke shall be destroyed
because of the anointing" (Isaiah 10:27). What is the
anointing? It is that supernatural, energizing force within
that makes the Spirit-filled life forcible, effective, and
productive in Christian service. How do you get it? "But

the anointing which ye have received of him abideth in you" (1 John 2:27). If you're a Christian, it abides in you.

Jesus was the Anointed One as He walked on this earth. "The Spirit of the Lord is upon me, because he hath anointed me to preach the gospel to the poor; he hath sent me to heal the broken-hearted, to preach deliverance to the captives, and recovering of sight to the blind, to set at liberty them that are bruised, To preach the acceptable year of the Lord" (Luke 4:18, 19).

All of the miracles which Jesus performed while He was here on earth were done through the power of His anointing. "God anointed Jesus of Nazareth with the Holy Ghost and with power: who went about doing good, and healing all that were oppressed of the devil; for God was with him" (Acts 10:38).

The anointing is the quality which makes us dynamic for the Lord. It enables us to see Christ-like results in our lives. It gives us authority to speak in the name of Jesus against satanic powers — all satanic powers, not just the powers that cause depression.

Psalm 92:10 says, "I shall be anointed with fresh oil." The anointing of the Holy Spirit is likened in Scripture to oil. Oil is a type, or "word picture," of the Holy Spirit. On the Day of Pentecost the disciples were all filled with the Holy Ghost (Acts 2:4). Later these same disciples were again filled with the Holy Ghost (Acts 4:29-31). Like the disciples, we too need fresh anointings and infillings of the Holy Spirit.

Jude 20 says, "But ye, beloved, building up yourselves on your most holy faith, praying in the Holy

Ghost." Fervent, anointed prayer in the Holy Ghost builds up our faith.

"But ye have an unction from the Holy One ... " (1 John 2:20). We should cherish this anointing, this unction that abides within us, and daily yield to the Holy Spirit to impart fresh oil to us.

How do you cope with depression? It is the anointing that breaks the yoke! We can maintain the anointing and overcome depression by a life rich with fellowship with the Lord.

How To Cope with Insomnia

Are you troubled with insomnia? Do you lie awake and restless some of the night — every night?

In millions of beds there is a nightly battle. It's the power of God versus the power of Satan. Since God is the author of sleep, a good and necessary gift, then Satan in the author of insomnia. Satan seeks to steal your sleep, thereby destroying your health, peace, and well-being. Sleeplessness breeds nervous disorders, depression, stress, and many kinds of illness.

If you suffer from insomnia, there is a promise in God's Word for you: "He giveth his beloved sleep" (Psalm 127:2). Therefore, you have a sure cure for sleeplessness: you can rout Satan and sleeplessness the way Jesus defeated the devil — by declaring, "it is written."

Take your sleep, not by counting sheep, but by quoting God's wonderful Word.

Say, "Devil, IT IS WRITTEN that God gives His beloved sleep, according to Psalm 127:2!"

Say, "Devil, IT IS WRITTEN that I will both lay me down in peace, and sleep: for the Lord makes me dwell in safety according to Psalm 4:8!"

Say, "Devil, IT IS WRITTEN that when I lie down, I shall not be afraid: yea, I shall lie down and my sleep shall be sweet, according to Proverbs 4:26!"

Peace is a prerequisite for sleep. Before lying down at night, through prayer and praise remove from your mind all anxieties, grudges, resentments, failures, and disappointments. "Be careful for nothing; but in everything by prayer and supplication with thanksgiving let your requests be made known unto God. And the peace of God, which passeth all understanding, shall keep your hearts and minds through Christ Jesus" (Philippians 4:6, 7).

As you cast your cares upon Him, you will find peace. Then you will find it will be easy to go to sleep, free from fear and anxiety in the knowledge that God is watching over you and everything that pertains to you.

How to Cope with Stress

Stress is a common denominator among people in all strata of today's society. Everyone is concerned about stress. Best-selling books deal with the subject. Courses are taught about it. Businesses are concerned about the toil it takes on the health and productivity of its employees.

In addition to being a drastically wearing force on our mental and physical functions, stress is actually a killer. It has been discovered to be associated with such maladies as ulcers, heart disease, and even cancer.

Is it possible for the Christian to live free from stress with the world in the shape it's in today? With rapes, muggings, robbery, murder and disaster threatening us daily? With crises in the economy and the specter of nuclear destruction ever before us?

God's Word has an antidote for stress: "Thou wilt keep him in perfect peace, whose mind is stayed on thee" (Isaiah 26:3).

Instead of worrying that someone in your family will be the victim of rape, robbery, muggings or murder, AIDS, herpes, heart attack or cancer, stand in the power of God's Word which says, "The angel of the Lord encampeth round about them that fear him, and delivereth them" (Psalm 34:7). Say, "Devil, IT IS WRITTEN that no evil shall befall me, neither shall any plague come nigh my dwelling!" (Psalm 91:10).

Instead of worrying about problems on your job, claim the promise of God which says, "The Lord shall fight for you, and ye shall hold your peace" (Exodus 14:14). Say, "Devil, IT IS WRITTEN that the Lord shall deliver me from every evil work!" (2 Timothy 4:18). Say, "Devil, IT IS WRITTEN that when the enemy shall come in like a flood, the Spirit of the Lord shall lift up a standard against him!" (Isaiah 59:19). Remember that God's Spirit is raising a mighty standard of defense in your behalf at the very time others might be putting pressure on you. The battle is not yours, but God's (2 Chronicles 20:15).

Instead of worrying about how to pay your bills, quote God's promise that "My God shall supply all your need according to his riches in glory by Christ Jesus" (Philippians 4:19). Turn all your cares and worries over to the Lord, "Casting all you care upon him, for he careth for you" (1 Peter 5:7).

The Bible says, "Commit thy way unto the Lord; trust also in him; and he shall bring it to pass" (Psalm 37:5). When you fully commit your life to God and place your trust in Him, He will work out every detail of your life.

How to Cope with Indecision

A major cause of unhappiness, frustration, tension, and failure is the inability to make a clear-cut decision. It has been said, "The world turns aside to let any man pass who knows where he is going." But how can we achieve this confidence in decision-making? Can good judgment be acquired? Can we learn how to make the right decision every time?

Certainly life is much better for the one who learns to make up his mind. Jesus came "to guide our feet into the way of peace" (Luke 1:79). God's clear promise in His Word is that He will help you with life's decisions. "If any of you lack wisdom, let him ask of God, that giveth to all men liberally, and upbraideth not; and it shall be given him" (James 1:5).

As Spirit-filled believers, we can expect to be Spirit-led as well, for we have access to supernatural guidance: "Howbeit when he, the Spirit of truth, is come, he will guide you into all truth: for he shall not speak of himself; but whatsoever he shall hear, that shall he speak: and he will show you things to come" (John 16:13).

Prayer is helpful in making a right decision. Tell the Lord that you want to do the right thing; tell Him that if He will show you what it is, you will do it regardless of the cost. "And thine ears shall hear a word behind thee, saying, This is the way, walk ye in it, when ye turn to the right hand, and when ye turn to the left" (Isaiah 30:21). "For this God is our God for ever and ever: he will be our guide even unto death" (Psalm 48:14).

If you expect to succeed, you have to be someone who can make decisions, who can take some chances, and go on. Don't vacillate. When you have a decision to make, seek God. Then make your decision and go ahead. When James promised wisdom to any man who asked for it, he cautioned, "But let him ask in faith, nothing wavering. For he that wavereth is like a wave of the sea driven with the wind and tossed. For let not that man think that he shall receive any thing of the Lord. A double minded man is unstable in all his ways" (James 1:6-8). You may make mistakes, but no more than if you dilly-dally around.

The ability to make up your mind inspires self-confidence, gives you inner power, and commands the respect of your fellow men. "Thou shalt guide me with thy counsel, and afterward receive me to glory" (Psalm 73:24).

Many marriages have ended in divorce merely because one or both parties never fully, completely, and irrevocably decided that this was the partner they wanted for life. One should never enter into marriage without having reached such a decision, without making a firm lifetime commitment.

Many questions can be settled with just one decision: the decision to go God's way. The question of honesty is a case in point. One should decide once and for all whether he intends to be honest. Then the temptation to dishonesty is never a problem. The psalmist declared:

"I hate and abhor lying: but thy law do I love" (Psalm 119:163).

Another decision we can make in advance is the matter of giving to the Lord our tithes and offerings. Then when we are faced with a challenge to give, there's no struggle in indecision, for we know God's Word says:

"Give, and it shall be given unto you; good measure, pressed down, and shaken together, and running over, shall men give into your bosom. For with the same measure that ye mete withal it shall be measured to you again" (Luke 6:38).

Remember, God has committed Himself in His Word to guide and direct your life according to His perfect plan.

"I will instruct thee and teach thee in the way which thou shalt go; I will guide thee with mine eye" (Psalm 32:18).

RX for Action:

In order to resist the devil and have him flee from you, you must:

1. Detect the devil's devices.

2. Disagree with the devil by agreeing with God's Word.

3. Dislodge the demons by dominion in Jesus' name.

4. Discharge the demonical device by boldly quoting the Word.

You Can Defeat the Devil

When you are attacked by "the devil's D's" of defeat, discouragement, destruction, desolation, distress, and despair, grab your "shield of faith, wherewith ye shall be able to quench all the fiery darts of the wicked" (Ephesians 6:16). But don't stay on the defensive. The next step is to reach for your "sword of the Spirit, which is the word of God" (Ephesians 6:17) and "Fight the good fight of faith" (2 Timothy 6:12). Here are some Scriptures that will help you defeat his demonical devices!

He delivereth the poor in his affliction, and openeth their ears in oppression.

JOB 36:15

The LORD also will be a refuge for the oppressed, a refuge in times of trouble.
                    PSALM 9:9

There shall no strange god be in thee...
                    PSALM 81:9

Let the redeemed of the LORD say so, whom he hath redeemed from the hand of the enemy.
                    PSALM 107:2

For ever, O LORD, thy word is settled in heaven.
                    PSALM 119:89

Be surety for thy servant for good: let not the proud oppress me.
                    PSALM 119:122

Order my steps in thy word: and let not any iniquity have dominion over me.
                    PSALM 119:133

If the Son therefore shall make you free, ye shall be free indeed.
                    JOHN   8:36

How God anointed Jesus of Nazareth with the Holy Ghost and with power: who went about doing good, and healing all that were oppressed of the devil; for God was with him.
                    ACTS 10:38

(For the weapons of our warfare are not carnal, but mighty through God to the pulling down of strongholds;) Casting down imaginations, and every high thing that exalteth itself against the knowledge of God, and bringing into captivity every thought to the obedience of Christ.

2 CORINTHIANS 10:4, 5

And they overcame him by the blood of the Lamb, and by the word of their testimony; and they loved not their lives unto the death.

REVELATION 12:19

Chapter Nine

How to Cope With Pride

One morning in January, 1976, I awakened with a splitting headache. Now headaches are something I've never had, so it was a new area of life for me. As the day continued on, I thought, "Never having experienced a headache has caused me to have little compassion for those people who suffer with migraines."

Frankly, I expected that "time would heal" and the headache would simply fade away. But the next morning the headache was still very much a part of my life. I went through the usual procedures in prayer, asking God to heal me.

I was soon to learn that time was not the healer of these headaches, for they stubbornly persisted through an entire week. With each passing day, the pain was more severe.

After seven days of enduring this affliction, I really got down to business with the Lord. I boldly spoke the Word, resisted the devil, praised the Lord, acted my faith, and took all the steps I had taken in receiving previous healings from the Lord.

All the second week, I took my stand in faith and fully expected the healing power of Jesus to make me whole.

After two weeks had passed, the headaches were more a part of my life than ever. So I decided to consult my family doctor about the problem. He prescribed a certain popular medicine, which I purchased and took according to directions.

When I became aware that the medicine wasn't helping, I decided to try another headache remedy I heard advertised on television. During the third week of my suffering, none of these medications was helping.

As the fourth week came and went, I discovered that I wasn't thinking about winning lost souls. I wasn't focusing on compassionate prayers for the sick. All I could think about was my wretched headache! I was walking around feeling less than a human, and wondering how long I could survive this horrible condition.

When the 30th day arrived, we were overseas in a crusade and were invited by a school superintendent and his wife to go sightseeing. We had lunch at a lovely hotel and saw pleasant sights. But I was simply enduring all the hospitality of these friends. It was the worst day of the 30 since the headaches had occurred.

Falling into bed that night, I announced to my wife, "Honey, I don't want to go on living like this. I would rather die than live with this severe pain." I was feeling quite sorry for myself, which didn't help anything.

When I arose the next morning, I further informed Joyce, "Honey, I can't go through another month like the last one has been. God has got to help me. I am going into the little room at the back of this house where we are staying. I will lock myself in from the inside, and I will stay there until there is a manifestation of healing from the Lord."

I was never more determined in my life to meet God for a desperate need. I dropped on my knees and began to cry out to the Lord. I quickly identified with David in Psalm 34, "This poor man cried and the Lord heard him, and saved him out of all his troubles."

After less than an hour there on my knees, telling God all about the whole situation, I asked Him to show me reasons why the healing was not forthcoming.

Instantly I got an answer from God. He brought to my mind and spirit the words of James 4:6, "God resisteth the proud, but giveth grace unto the humble."

The Holy Spirit spoke to my heart, "One hundred times out of one hundred, I must resist you when you are proud, haughty, and arrogant. If you are praying and not receiving a definite answer, you need to search your heart to see if you have allowed pride to hinder the flow of My power into your life.

"If you are seeking healing, and the healing is not manifest, you need to examine your heart to see if you have permitted pride to come between Me and you.

"When you are in financial need, and the supply is not being granted, you should take stock on this matter of a spirit of pride hindering My supply of those needs."

Quickly I thumbed through my Bible and read these pertinent passages:

"Wherefore he saith, God resisteth the proud, but giveth grace unto the humble" (James 4:6).

"Be clothed with humility: for God resisteth the proud, and giveth grace to the humble. Humble yourself therefore under the mighty hand of God, that he may exalt you in due time" (1 Peter 5:5-6).

I knew that this was a principle found in both the Old and the New Testaments — that as long as we are proud, God must resist us.

Now I have known what it's like to be resisted by people, and that's difficult. I know what it's like to be resisted by my wife, and that's almost more than one can take. But to be resisted by God! That's critical. To be resisted by God means no answers to prayer, no healings manifested, no financial miracles. To be resisted by God is indeed "a high price for low living"!

Immediately I responded to this word from the Holy Spirit. I called out to God to forgive me for being proud and haughty, high-minded and arrogant.

What was God's reaction to my wholehearted confession? He forgave me! Praise His Name!

"If we confess our sins, he is faithful and just to forgive us our sins, and to cleanse us from all unrighteousness" (1 John 1:9).

I knew beyond the shadow of a doubt that I was completely forgiven, cleansed, restored, made whole. Having dealt with the hindering spirit of pride, I humbly continued in His presence. For the next 45 minutes, I alternately praised the Lord and confessed the Word aloud. I am persuaded that when you praise the Lord and confess the Word, nothing but good can come to you.

At the climax of those 45 glorious minutes of praise and confessing the Word, suddenly I had sort of a fading experience.

When I looked up, there stood a man in the room. My first reaction was, "This can't be! That door is locked from the inside. No one can get in this room."

As I held a steady gaze with this man, I noticed that his dress was somewhat out of character for this 20th century.

The man took steps towards me, then gently laid his hand upon my head. When he did so, it felt like warm oil flowing into my head. As this continued for a few moments, I was made aware that the pains of the severe headaches were all gone.

Then the man stepped back. My response to this vision was unusual. I cried out, "Sir, are you the Apostle Paul?"

I don't know why I asked such a question, but I was fully assured that this was a supernatural experience and I wanted my visitor to identify himself.

The man didn't answer immediately. Then he said, "I am an angel of the Lord sent to minister to you who are an heir of salvation."

Hebrews 1:14 flashed into my mind, that angels "are all ministering spirits, sent forth to minister for them who shall be heirs of salvation."

By the grace of God, that meant me! An heir of salvation. I was overjoyed by this divine visitation.

Suddenly the vision was over. The angel had vanished from the room. But I was the recipient of a beautiful miracle: the pain was still gone.

Wanting to make sure that the healing was real, I decided to wait 72 hours before telling my wife. When the headaches were still gone after 72 hours, I told Joyce. She rejoiced with me and urged me to share with the pastors with whom we were laboring. I did so, and they too rejoiced with us.

Some days later, we arrived home. The first morning we were home, the old pains came back with the same tenacity as before.

Joyce urged me to tell our children about the miracle healing and the vision. But the pains were back! I was dumbfounded and confused to the core.

The old devil whispered to me, "Uh, huh, you have told people you were healed of the headaches. You are the victim of my deception. Now you will suffer worse than ever."

It was a terrible, dark experience for me. I was a victim — a victim of satanic deception. But the Holy Spirit did not abandon me in that moment of extreme testing. He ministered comfort to me and brought this scripture forcibly to mind: "The thief cometh not but for to kill, to steal, and to destroy; I am come that they might have life and that they might have it more abundantly" (John 10:10).

Immediately I saw the true picture. Jesus had really healed me by His bleeding stripes. But now the thief was trying to steal my healing from me.

I arose in indignation. "Listen, devil, you are a liar. When I was visited by the angel, I was boldly speaking God's Word. Devil, you have tried to rob me of my healing by bringing back lying symptoms of the headaches. The actual headaches were healed by Jesus. Devil, I refuse to be your dumping ground. Take your old infirmities and go in Jesus' name. Devil, headaches are something I don't have anymore!"

Almost as instantly as the headaches had reoccurred, thank God they disappeared. That has been more than 10 years. What has happened about headaches? I am humbly thankful that I've never experienced a severe bout with headaches again. On rare occasion, there have been slight symptoms ... in my forehead, or the back of my head ... but I steadfastly resist them in Jesus' name.

"Devil, back off," I speak with indignation. "Headaches are something I don't have — Jesus made me whole!"

Once, when small head distress persisted for a few minutes, I boldly announced to the devil, "Listen, Satan, if you try to afflict me with headaches, next time God may dispatch a legion of angels to minister to me!"

I learned one very forcible lesson from that whole experience: There is no room in the Christian life for a spirit of pride. Such a spirit stops the flow of God's power within us.

Jesus' disciples were bothered by this spirit of pride. "Then there arose a reasoning among them, which of them should be the greatest" (Luke 9:46). Jesus told them, "He that is least among you all, the same shall be great" (verse 48). On another occasion, Jesus said,

"Whosoever exalteth himself shall be abased; and he that humbleth himself shall be exalted" (Luke 14:11).

I know from experience that pride is a sin that slips up on us unaware: take a moment now to ask God to show you if this is something that needs to be dealt with in you own life. If heaven's searchlight has pointed out a spirit of pride within your heart, pray with the psalmist, "Create in me a clean heart, O God; and renew a right spirit within me" (Psalm 51:10).

I am deeply grateful for God's miraculous healing of my headaches. I expect never to be so oppressed again, because God showed me, through it, the principles that He will honor in manifesting His healing power.

RX for Action:

The spirit of pride is devastating, because it cuts off the flow of God's blessing in our lives. As long as pride is prevalent in our hearts, God has to resist us. When your prayers aren't answered, ask the Lord: Am I harboring pride in my heart?

In those wonderful 45 minutes before the healing was fully manifested, I "kept heaven busy" responding to me as I praised the Lord and affirmed His Word. Praising the Lord and confessing His promises will always bring results when our hearts are right with Him.

Finally, I learned to discern what was of God and what was of Satan. Satan will often try to steal the blessings God has given you — that's why he's called "the thief"! When the devil attempted to steal my healing from me, by the grace of God I was "not ignorant of his devices" and rose up and refused to allow my body to be his dumping ground any longer. Resisting the devil is an important part of receiving and keeping God's blessings.

Scriptures Concerning Pride

Pride is a spirit — an evil one. As such, the best way to fight it is with "the sword of the Spirit, which is the word of God." This is the same weapon Jesus fought with, when He was tempted by the devil in the wilderness, and we can use it exactly the same way He did. When the devil comes against you in this area, simply say, 'Devil, IT IS WRITTEN ... ' — and then quote one or more scriptures that are appropriate to the situation. Here are a few to start you off:

The LORD shall cut off ... the tongue that speaketh proud things: Who have said, With our tongue will we prevail; our lips are our own: who is lord over us?

PSALM 12:3, 4

Thou wilt save the afflicted people: but will bring down high looks.

PSALM 18:27

Him that hath an high look and proud heart will not I suffer.

PSALM 101:5

Thou hast rebuked the proud that are cursed, which do err from thy commandments.

PSALM 119:21

Though the LORD be high, yet hath he respect unto the lowly: but the proud he knoweth afar off.

PSALM 138:6

Surely he scorneth the scorners: but he giveth grace unto the lowly.

PROVERBS 3:34

When pride cometh, then cometh shame; but with the lowly is wisdom.

PROVERBS 11:2

Only by pride cometh contention.

PROVERBS 13:10

He that despiseth his neighbor sinneth.

PROVERBS 14:21

Every one that is proud in heart is an abomination to the LORD: though hand join in hand, he shall not be unpunished.

PROVERBS 16:5

Pride goeth before destruction, and an haughty spirit before a fall.

PROVERBS 16:18

Let another man praise thee, and not thine own mouth; a stranger, and not thine own lips.
PROVERBS 27:2

Let not the wise man glory in his wisdom, neither let the mighty man glory in his might, let not the rich man glory in his riches: But let him that glorieth glory in this, that he understandeth and knoweth me, that I am the LORD which exercise lovingkindness, judgment and righteousness, in the earth: for in these things I delight, saith the LORD.
JEREMIAH 9:23, 24

Because thou hast trusted in thy works and in thy treasures, thou shalt also be taken.
JEREMIAH   48:7

Behold, this was the iniquity of thy sister Sodom, pride, fullness of bread, and abundance of idleness was in her and in her daughter, neither did she strengthen the hand of the poor and needy.
EZEKIEL 16:49

Woe unto you, Pharisees! for ye love the uppermost seats in the synagogues, and greetings in the markets.
LUKE 11:43

Charity vaunteth not itself, is not puffed up.
1 CORINTHIANS 13:4

If a man think himself to be something, when he is nothing, he deceiveth himself.

GALATIANS 6:3

Let nothing be done through strife or vain glory; but in lowliness of mind let each esteem the other better than themselves.

PHILIPPIANS 2:3

Wherefore he saith, God resisteth the proud, but giveth grace to the humble.

JAMES 4:6

All that is in the world, the lust of the flesh, and the lust of the eyes, and the pride of life, is not of the Father, but is of the world.

1 JOHN 2:16

Because thou sayest, I am rich, and increased with goods, and have need of nothing; and knowest not that thou art wretched, and miserable, and poor, and blind, and naked: I counsel thee to buy of me gold tried in the fire, that thou mayest be rich; and white raiment, that thou mayest be clothed, and that the shame of thy nakedness do not appear: and anoint thine eyes with eyesalve, that thou mayest see.

REVELATION 3:17, 18

Chapter Ten

How to Cope With Fear, Pessimism, Inadequacy and Inferiority

In the last chapter, we looked at how to defeat the devil's devices. In this chapter, I want to expose four more of his strongholds: feelings of fear, pessimism, inadequacy, and inferiority. Actually, these are all related, for they all stem from believing the things that the devil is whispering in your ear instead of believing what the Word of God clearly states about your situation.

How to Cope With Fear

Fear has one source: the devil. "For God hath not given us a spirit of fear; but of power, and of love, and of a sound mind" (2 Timothy 1:7). I want you to notice that according to the Word of God, fear is not a mental quirk. It is not an imagination or a feeling, but an actual spirit that is given to us, not by God, but by Satan.

The results of fear are not pleasant. In fact, the Bible says that "fear hath torment" (1 John 4:18). Victims of

113

fear often suffer physical agony, mental anguish, and spiritual torment.

Furthermore, fear is deceptive. Because of fear, people will rush into traps that are laid for them by the devil. "The fear of man bringeth a snare" (Proverbs 29:15). Fear leads astray, beguiles, deludes.

Fear produces in kind, just as faith produces in kind. If you believe God will heal you — He will! If you fear the devil will afflict you with cancer — he will! Thus the fear of disease can actually produce disease; the fear of calamity can actually bring that calamity upon you; fear failure, and you open the door for failure to engulf your life. This is what happened to Job: "For the thing which I greatly feared is come upon me, and that which I was afraid of is come unto me" (Job 3:25). Defeat, depression, disease, destruction, and even death were the result of Job's fears.

Fear is destructive, leading some even to the brink of suicide. Fear causes sleeplessness, nervous breakdowns, oppression in your prayer life, and bondage in witnessing.

Fear causes you to expect the worst.

Dare to rebuke fear in the name of Jesus. Call the author of fear by his right name: deceiver, liar, fraud. "Resist the devil, and he will flee from you" (James 4:7).

A woman in Sydney, British Columbia, who had been a victim of fear, wrote to tell me: "Before I heard your radio broadcast, fear used to grip me like a vise no matter where I went. I prayed always for God's help and I know He answered by leading me to listen to your broadcast. Now I've learned how to cast out all fear in the name of Jesus. I'm trusting God completely now and am a positive Christian. I thank the Lord for using you in this way."

And a friend of mine in Moose Jaw, Saskatchewan, wrote: "Your messages on fear are helpful and interesting. So many people have phobias and superstitions about this and that, as you describe, and they make life difficult for themselves and others. So your message on this subject must do an immense amount of good to those who are in bondage to such beliefs. I trust that many will be persuaded to turn their problems over to God and find deliverance."

Because God is with you, you need no longer fear. "Fear thou not; for I am with thee: be not dismayed; for I am thy God: I will strengthen thee; yea, I will help thee; yea, I will uphold thee with the right hand of my righteousness" (Isaiah 41:10).

How to Cope with a Pessimistic Attitude

Pessimism is nothing more nor less than unbelief. If you truly believe what God says in His Word, you will be an optimist, not a pessimist.

The Bible reveals that when you were born again, you were not destined to defeat. You were actually born to conquer. "Nay, in all these things we are more than conquerors through him that loved us" (Romans 8:37).

God's Word says that you are not just a conqueror, you are MORE than a conqueror! When you enter a battle, you don't win a pyrrhic victory; you overwhelmingly defeat the enemy.

We've heard it said that when the going gets tough, the tough get going. So shake off that feeling of defeat, and get yourself going. God is for you. "What shall we then say to these things? If God be for us, who can be against us?" (Romans 8:31).

In Joshua 1:2-9 we read God's formula for victory and success. Our part: "Arise go over ... be strong and of a good courage ... be not afraid, neither be thou dismayed." God's part: "I will be with thee: I will not fail thee, nor forsake thee." The result: "Then thou shalt make thy way prosperous, and then thou shalt have good success."

In case you think that God's promise to be with Joshua was only addressed to him, I can assure you that we have the very same promise given to all believers in the New Testament. Jesus said, "and lo, I am with you alway, even unto the end of the world" (Matthew 28:20).

You can turn your defeated, pessimistic outlook on your life into an overcoming, faith-filled "uplook." Reverse your thinking. CHANGE YOUR VOCABULARY.

Instead of saying, "I can't get my prayers answered," say, "According to God's Word, This is my confidence toward God, that 'whatsoever we ask, we receive of him, because we keep his commandments, and do those things that are pleasing in his sight' " (1 John 3:21, 22).

Instead of saying, "My loved ones won't serve the Lord," declare, "According to Acts 16:31, 'Believe on the Lord Jesus Christ, and thou shalt be saved, and thy house,' I believe for the salvation of my household!"

Instead of saying, "I can't receive my healing," confess that "By His stripes, I am healed" (Isaiah 53:5).

Begin to talk victory, not defeat. Act like a conqueror, for in Christ you ARE one!

How to Cope with Feelings of Inadequacy

Psychologists may talk about "feelings of inadequacy"; I call it "I-Can't-itis."

You can remove the destructive words "I can't" from your vocabulary forever. Search the Scriptures: nowhere in the Bible is there any indication that there is anything that you or I cannot accomplish. Instead, Philippians 4:13 says, "I CAN DO all things through Christ which strengtheneth me."

Ask the Holy Spirit to correct you whenever you are tempted to say, "I can't." Instead, speak God's language. Say what His Word says. Harmonize with heaven by affirming God's Word. Agree with God by agreeing with His Word.

Resolve now never again to say, "I can't receive my healing," for with his stripes you are healed. You CAN receive your healing because Jesus said, "These signs shall follow them that believe ... they shall lay hands on the sick, and they shall recover" (Mark 16:17, 18).

Resolve now never again to say, "I can't pay my bills," since Philippians 4:19 says, "But my God shall supply all your need according to his riches in glory by Christ Jesus." Therefore you can say, "I CAN pay my bills because my God supplies the money to meet every need in my life."

Resolve now not to say, "I can't witness. When I have a chance to give my testimony, I can't think of what to say." Instead, proclaim that you CAN witness through the power of the Holy Spirit, since Acts 1:8 says, "But ye shall receive power, after that the Holy Ghost is come upon you: and ye shall be witnesses unto me ... " Say, "I CAN share my testimony with great effectiveness because I am energized by the mighty Holy Ghost from heaven."

Above all else, make a firm commitment to yourself that you will never again say, "I just can't get my prayers answered." This kind of statement will close the doors of heaven to your life, since the Bible clearly teaches in Mark 11:23, 24 that what you say is what you get. Instead, speak out with assurance, saying, "I CAN receive the answer to my prayers, since Jesus said in several places that whatever I would ask in His name, He would do." I CAN receive mighty answers from God, for He has promised "Call unto me, and I will answer thee, and shew thee great and mighty things, which thou knowest not" (Jeremiah 33:3).

Also very important is your decision not to agree with the devil by saying, "I can't see my loved ones won to Christ," since God's Word clearly states that "this is my covenant with them, saith the LORD; My spirit that is upon thee, and my words which I have put in thy mouth, shall not depart out of thy mouth, nor out of the mouth of thy seed, nor out of the mouth of thy seed's seed, saith the LORD, henceforth and for ever" (Isaiah 59:21). When the children of Israel celebrated passover, the Old Testament rule was "a lamb for an house"

(Exodus 12:3). This was to symbolize the New Testament truth, "Believe on the Lord Jesus Christ, and thou shalt be saved, and thy house" (Acts 16:31). Now that you know this, you can boldly say, "I CAN see all my loved ones saved because I am God's instrument to believe for their salvation!"

Even in personal matters, never say "I Can't." Don't let "I-Can't-itis" attack anything that concerns you, for Psalm 138:8 declares, "The LORD will perfect that which concerneth me." Does your weight concern you? Don't say, "I can't seem to stick on a diet." Instead say, "I CAN do all things through Christ, and God will perfect that which concerns me." Are you having trouble with your co-workers? Don't say, "I can't seem to get along with So-and-so." Instead affirm, "I have favor with So-and-so. 'For thou, LORD will bless the righteous; with favour wilt thou compass him as with a shield,' according to Psalm 5:12." Once you get your words in line with God's Word, you will be surprised at how quickly feelings of inadequacy leave you. Yes, it's true, without God you're a loser — and so are all of us. But with God on your side there is nothing that you cannot do. For a Christian, feelings of inadequacy are exactly that: just feelings. They do not reflect the true state of reality, which is that you and God are more than adequate in any situation.

How to Cope with an Inferiority Complex

Closely related to "I-Can't-itis" is what some psychologists have called an "inferiority complex."

As a born-again Christian, you are in Christ and Christ is in you. The very word "Christian" means we are "Christ-in" people. We're not "Christian workers." We are "Christ containers."

There can be absolutely nothing inferior about you because there is nothing inferior about Christ — and you contain Him. Sixty-seven different times in the writings of Paul alone, the Bible tells us that we are *in Christ* if we are born again.

How can you be inferior when "ye are dead, and your life is hid with Christ in God" (Colossians 3:3)?

If you were a king's son, or a king's daughter, would you feel inferior? Yet you are a child of the King of Kings! How can you feel inferior when you are the apple of God's eye — and He created everything there is?

You may feel that you are insufficient in some area, and — in the natural — you may be right. But the Word of God says "our sufficiency is of God" (2 Corinthians 3:5). You need not worry about what you can or cannot do, for God IN YOU can do everything!

Christianity is a "say-so" way of life. Psalm 107:2 says, "Let the redeemed of the Lord SAY SO"! This is how you became a Christian in the first place: "With the mouth confession is made unto salvation" (Romans 10:10). Your mouth makes confession "unto salvation," not only when you are born again, but also whenever you operate according to Mark 11:23, 24. You cannot rise higher than your confession. A wrong confession will imprison you; a right confession will set you free.

What are we to say? Again and again I repeat that we should say what God says, for God's Word is truth. It doesn't matter what we think, feel, or see: what does matter is what God has told us in His Word.

Joel 3:10 says, "Let the weak say, I am strong." Therefore, confess that you are strong — whether you feel strong or not. Say, "In obedience to Joel 3:10, I say I'm strong."

What is the area in which the devil would try to weaken you? Do you feel defeated? Say, "Now thanks be unto God, which always causeth us to triumph in Christ" (2 Corinthians 2:14). Do you feel apologetic? Say, "I know whom I have believed, and am persuaded that he is able to keep that which I have committed unto him against that day" (2 Timothy 1:12). Do you feel timid? Say, "If God be for us, who can be against us?" (Romans 8:31).

As you allow Christ to live His life in you, you can overcome your inferiority complex by a joyful awareness that it is, "not I, but Christ [Who] liveth in me" (Galatians 2:20).

RX for Action:

REBUKE the devil in the name of Jesus. "And the seventy returned again with joy, saying, Lord, even the devils are subject unto us THROUGH THY NAME" (Luke 10:17). It is only through the name of Jesus that we have the power to take authority over spirits of fear, pessimism, inadequacy, and inferiority.

REMEMBER that in Christ, you are "more than a conqueror."

REVISE your vocabulary. Delete anything negative. Acquire a "can-do" attitude, because you CAN do all things — through Christ.

REALIZE who you are in Christ.

REAFFIRM the positive, and REJECT the negative through the use of appropriate Scriptures.

Fear Thou Not

We think of it as a shortcoming, or an inconvenience, or a torment; but actually, fear is a sin. Revelation 21:8 says, "But the fearful, and unbelieving, and the abominable, and murderers, and whoremongers, and sorcerers, and idolaters, and all liars, shall have their part in the lake which burneth with fire and brimstone: which is the second death."

Do you think murder is bad? Fear is listed in Revelation 21:8 before murder. Do you think managing a house of prostitution is bad? The fearful are listed before whoremongers. Do you think sorcery and idolatry are bad? Fear must be just as bad, because it heads the list!

Fear is a serious sin. I tell you this, not to scare you even more than ever, but so that you can repent. "If we confess our sins, he is faithful and just to forgive us our sins, and to cleanse us from all unrighteousness" (1 John

1:9). After you repent and confess the sin of fear, stand on the following Scriptures:

Have not I commanded thee? Be strong and of a good courage: be not afraid, neither be thou dismayed; for the LORD thy God is with thee withersoever thou goest.

JOSHUA 1:9

Yea, though I walk through the valley of the shadow of death, I will fear no evil: for thou art with me.

PSALM 23:4

The LORD is my light and my salvation; whom shall I fear? the LORD is the strength of my life; of whom shall I be afraid?

PSALM 27:1

Though an host should encamp against me, my heart shall not fear ...

PSALM 27:3

God is our refuge and strength, a very present help in trouble. Therefore will we not fear, though the earth be removed, and though the mountains be carried into the midst of the sea.

PSALM 46:1, 2

He sent his word, and healed them, and delivered them from their destructions.

PSALM 107:20

The LORD is on my side; I will not fear: what can man do unto me?

PSALM 118:6

The fear of the wicked, it shall come upon him: But the desire of the righteous shall be granted.

PROVERBS 10:24

Thou wilt keep him in perfect peace, whose mind is stayed on thee: because he trusteth in thee.

ISAIAH 26:3

For the Lord GOD will help me; therefore shall I not be confounded: therefore have I set my face like a flint, and I know that I shall not be ashamed.

ISAIAH 50:7

When the enemy shall come in like a flood, the Spirit of the LORD shall lift up a standard against him.

ISAIAH 59:19

Fear ye not therefore, ye are of more value than many sparrows.

MATTHEW 10:31

But we have the mind of Christ.

1 CORINTHIANS 2:16

Now thanks be unto God, which always causeth us to triumph in Christ, and maketh manifest the savor of his knowledge by us in every place.

2 CORINTHIANS 2:14

For God hath not given us the spirit of fear; but of power, and of love, and of a sound mind.

2 TIMOTHY 1:7

For this purpose the Son of God was manifested, that he might destroy the works of the devil.

1 JOHN 3:8

Ye are of God, little children, and have overcome them: because greater is he that is in you, than he that is in the world.

1 JOHN 4:4

There is no fear in love; but perfect love casteth out fear: because fear hath torment. He that feareth is not made perfect in love.

1 JOHN 4:18

Chapter Eleven

How to Cope
With Sickness

"If she were my wife, Rev. Gossett, I would never allow her to go to an undeveloped country like India!"

Those were the words of a specialist at the City of Faith in Tulsa, Oklahoma. He had just given my wife, Joyce, a thorough examination of a severe hemorrhoid problem with which she was suffering great pain.

That was in December, 1982, just six weeks before our scheduled departure for crusades in India. We respected the advise of the specialist and seriously considered Joyce having surgery for her critical hemorrhoid problem.

As we spent the rest of that day making our decision, a foremost thought was that Christmas was only days ahead, and staying there would mean that Joyce might miss being home for Christmas with our family.

We informed the doctor of our decision and left Tulsa to fly west to our home.

Joyce continued to suffer much with the internal condition. But when it came time to leave for India, we prayerfully decided to take a bold "step of faith" ... Joyce would accompany me to India.

It was in India that God's power was miraculously manifested and the Lord made Joyce every whit whole! Praise the Lord, that was the end of her hemorrhoid suffering and condition.

The miracle happened in January, 1983. Later that year, we returned to Tulsa for the annual Health Appraisal that Oral Roberts invited us to do each year.

How happy this same specialist was when he examined her again, and discovered that the Lord had made Joyce completely whole!

When I review the past years in my "five-years diary," I recorded many entries of nights awake when Joyce was experiencing the torments of the damned with her hemorrhoid condition. Thank God for the victory ... Joyce has never suffered a day or night since the healing in India in January, 1983!

A woman in Sydney, British Columbia, wrote, "I was very ill and could hardly pray. Satan was putting pressure on me as I was learning to praise the Lord. I went to bed and decided to praise the Lord all night, and I did. All night long I said, 'Praise the Lord, for He is good, for His mercy endureth forever.' In the morning I was still praising the Lord, and the terrible headache and other ailments in my body were all gone. I felt as good as new when I got up. Thanks be to our mighty God who inhabits our praises."

A woman in Montserrat, West Indies, wrote: "When I read your book, *Praise Power,* I began praising God by faith for my healing, and the Lord healed me completely. It was a real answer to prayer and praise."

Healing is a gift of God. It has always been a gift, not something earned or deserved. First Corinthians 12 informs us that the "gifts of healing" are among the nine gifts of the Spirit. God has put the gifts of healing in the church, and no one can take these gifts away.

Healing is yours because of the provision of Jesus Christ. "But he was wounded for our transgressions, he was bruised for our iniquities: the chastisement of our peace was upon him; and with his stripes we are healed" (Isaiah 53:5). It is therefore scriptural to say, "I was healed over 1,900 years ago." Healing is a finished work. It is an accomplished fact. Jesus has already paid for it.

Healing is a gift appropriated by faith only. Jesus often said to those to whom He ministered, "Thy faith hath made thee whole." It is faith that ministers healing, and the language of faith is praise.

Some mistakes people make in seeking healing are:

(1) Putting healing off until the future. *Jesus has already healed you.* By your faith you can appropriate that healing NOW.

(2) Begging God over and over to do it. God WANTS you well. I don't care if you have a well-deserved case of AIDS: 2 Chronicles 20:9 says, "If, when evil cometh upon us, as the sword, JUDGMENT, or pestilence, or famine, we stand before this house, and in thy presence, (for thy name is in this house,) and cry

unto thee in our affliction, then thou wilt hear and help."
God is a God "Who forgiveth all thine iniquities; who
healeth all thy diseases" (Psalm 103:3). He says to you,
"Beloved, I wish above all things that thou mayest
prosper and be in health, even as thy soul prospereth."
Begging God to heal you when He has already promised
to do so is nothing but a symptom of a lack of faith.

(3) Trying to get enough faith is another mistake.
Romans 12:3 reveals that "God hath dealt to every man
the measure of faith," and Jesus said that "If ye have
faith as a grain of mustard seed, ye shall say unto this
mountain, Remove hence to yonder place; and it shall
remove; and nothing shall be impossible unto you"
(Matthew 17:20). If you are a born-again believer, you
already have all the faith required — all you need to do
now is use it!

(4) Fasting for a long time can also be a mistake,
depending on WHY you're fasting. Healing is a gift.
God doesn't heal us because we deserve to be healed,
any more than He saves us because we deserve to be
saved. We cannot earn the gifts of God by fasting.

Healing is merely a matter of believing God's
Word, accepting it, applying it to your need, and acting
on it. We must always remember that salvation and
healing are already provided for. They already belong to
us: therefore we don't have to beg God for them. We
just receive these gifts by faith. It does no good to beg
God to do what He has clearly already done. Jesus bore
His stripes once and for all: He doesn't have to suffer
that punishment again. It is a completed work, and "with
his stripes we are healed" (Isaiah 53:5).

You don't need to say, "I feel no different." Jesus
didn't say, "according to your feelings," but "according
to your faith."

You don't need to say, "I know he is able, but ... "
He is exceeding abundantly able to heal you, according
to the power that is at work within you. Speak these
words: "By His power at work within me, He is healing
me now."

You don't need to say, "I hope I get my healing."
Hope is a beautiful thing when you are speaking of
heaven or the second coming of Christ. But hope is
always in the future. Faith is now. The "hoper" is
usually a failure. The believer is the winner. Declare,
"Lord, I believe!"

You don't need to say, "The disease I have is a
known killer." Instead of honoring your disease, honor
the greatest name ever spoken, the name of Jesus.
Exercise the authority of this name. There is miracle-
working power in the name of Jesus.

You don't need to say, "It's not the Lord's will for
me to be healed." Nowhere in the Bible does it indicate
that it is not God's will to heal everyone. People who
say it's not God's will to heal are usually the very ones
who are trying every natural means they know to get
well. If God doesn't want them well, why are they
seeing the doctor? Why are they taking medicine? No,
God's will is God's Word. His Word clearly reveals, "I
am the Lord that healeth thee" (Exodus 15:26).

You don't need to say, "I am suffering for the glory
of God." God is glorified more by your healing. Many

times in the Scripture we read, following the account of a healing, this statement: "And they glorified God."

You don't need to say, "I'm a truthful person, and I won't say, 'By His stripes I am healed,' until I know for sure I'm healed." What is truth? According to the Scriptures, "Thy Word is truth." Say what the Word says: "By His stripes I am healed."

Don't tell others in great detail about your sickness. This will, of course, gain sympathy and attention — but not healing. It will not only fuel your own discouragement, it will also discourage others who may need to trust God for their own healing and health.

Don't say, "When it comes to healing, I'm a real doubting Thomas. I have to be shown before I will ever believe." Also avoid such statements as, "It's so hard to believe God these days," or, "I have such little faith. I've tried trusting God, but it just doesn't work for me."

Don't say, "I must be like the Apostle Paul. I must have a thorn in the flesh. Paul prayed three times for it to be removed, but his request was denied. Therefore my illness must be my thorn in the flesh." Nowhere do the Scriptures tell us that Paul's thorn in the flesh was sickness. Rather, it was a messenger from Satan sent to buffet him because of the abundance of revelation that God had given him.

You have a right to be healed. But it is not because of anything you have done to merit it. Therefore, don't say, "I have a right to be healed because I have suffered so much." It is not because of your suffering, but because of Jesus' suffering that you have a right to healing. "Himself took our infirmities and bare our sicknesses" (Matthew 8:17).

Don't say, "I have a right to be healed because I have been a good, sincere person." It is not your goodness or sincerity that is your basis for healing. The blood of Jesus alone is your right to healing.

Don't say, "I have a right to be healed because I have attended church and Sunday School faithfully." To receive healing, you must depend entirely on the merits of Jesus Christ and not on anything you have done, however good.

Don't say, "I have a right to be healed because my family needs me so much." If that were the basis for healing, there would be no such thing as an orphan. Yes, your family needs you — but God has promised to heal you whether they need you or not, if you will only believe. To receive healing you must depend completely on the mediation of Jesus Christ, knowing that He provided healing by offering Himself in our stead.

Don't say, "I need healing so I may work for the Lord." God is able to raise up many workers. The only claim you have on healing is that JESUS CHRIST DIED TO PROVIDE IT FOR YOU. His blood alone qualifies you to receive it. You have been "made nigh by the blood of Jesus Christ" (Ephesians 2:13).

Yes, you have every right to be healed. But the only basis for that right is the substitutionary sacrifice of Christ himself.

Over the course of years, we have seen countless multitudes healed by the power of God. Here are a few more testimonies:

A woman in Antigua, West Indies, writes: "I sit close by my radio when you are on the air and I am blessed and refreshed by your words. We requested a prayer cloth based on Acts 19:11, 12, 'And God wrought special miracles by the hands of Paul; so that from his body were brought unto the sick handkerchiefs or aprons: and the diseases departed from them and the evil spirits went out of them.' I know that the God of Paul is our God today. I placed the prayer cloth on my body as my point of contact to receive my miracle. I am happy to report the pain is all gone. My husband then took the prayer cloth to a lady who loves God but who has been very sick. She did not send it back but kept it, and now she is up and about praising the Lord for His goodness to us all."

A man in Nevis, West Indies, writes: "Thank you for your encouragement. It's a great joy to listen to your broadcast over the air twice a day. I especially appreciated your message about healing. I claimed healing and used the words, 'By the stripes of Jesus I am healed.' The Lord has made me every whit whole and I praise His name."

A woman in Balmoral, Manitoba, writes: "I was saved and healed in my living room listening to you on the radio. I had been stricken with a condition in my right leg and could not help myself get out of bed or dress myself. One day I turned the radio on and you were just starting your sermon. I left it on to see what it was all about, and believe me, I was glad I did. I put my hand on the radio as you were praying for the sick, and the wonderful hand of Jesus touched me and I was healed instantly. That night I shut off the heat lamp and went to sleep without pain, and slept well. The next day I got up — after 11 months being in bed. It was wonderful to be up and around. I listen to you every day now and never miss it."

From a man and his wife in Terrace, British Columbia: "We want to tell you how wonderful the Lord was to us. We attended your meeting in Vancouver. It was after we had gone to an eye specialist in Victoria with our little girl. He had told us she was on the verge of losing her eyesight. That day we were the first ones up for prayer. The way the Lord led you to pray for our little girl without us ever telling you the trouble was marvelous. Right there and then we knew she was healed, praise God! A month later we took her back to the specialist, and he reported her eyes were 100 percent better. We give God all the glory."

RX for Action:

To receive your healing now:

1. Close your eyes and get a vision of Jesus enduring His stripes for you. Jesus did this for YOU.

2. Believe in your heart that you were healed over 1,900 years ago.

3. Confess it and possess it.

4. Praise the Lord that it is done.

5. Since it is done — act as if it is!

God Wants You Well

*"And this is the confidence we have in him," John
wrote, "that, if we ask any thing according to his will, he
heareth us: And if we know that he hear us, whatsoever
we ask, we know that we have the petitions that we
desired of him" (1 John 5:14, 15). Is it God's will to
heal you? The Bible clearly states that it is. Therefore, if
you ask for healing, He hears you — and since you
know He hears you, you know that He has said yes to
your petition!*

If thou wilt diligently hearken to the voice of the
LORD thy God, and wilt do that which is right in his
sight, and wilt give ear to his commandments, and keep
all his statutes, I will put none of these diseases upon
thee, which I have brought upon the Egyptians: for I am
the LORD that healeth thee.

EXODUS 15:26

And ye shall serve the LORD your God, and he
shall bless thy bread, and thy water; and I will take
sickness away from the midst of thee.

EXODUS 23:25

And the LORD will take away from thee all
sickness, and will put none of the evil diseases of Egypt,
which thou knowest, upon thee; but will lay them upon
all them that hate thee.

DEUTERONOMY 7:15

Surely he shall deliver thee from the snare of the
fowler, and from the noisome pestilence ... Thou shalt
not be afraid for the terror by night; nor for the arrow
that flieth by day; Nor for the pestilence that walketh in
darkness; nor the destruction that wasteth at noonday ...
Because he hath set his love upon me, therefore will I
deliver him: I will set him on high, because he hath
known my name. He shall call upon me, and I will
answer him: I will be with him in trouble; I will deliver
him, and honor him. With long life will I satisfy him,
and show Him my salvation.

PSALM 91:3, 5, 6, 14-16

Bless the LORD, O my soul, and forget not all his
benefits: Who forgiveth all thine iniquities, who healeth
all thy diseases.

PSALM 103:2, 3

He sent his word and healed them, and delivered
them from their destructions.

PSALM 107:20

My son, attend unto my words ... For they are life
unto those that find them, and health to all their flesh.

PROVERBS 4:20, 22

But he was wounded for our transgressions, he was
bruised for our iniquities: the chastisement of our peace
was upon him; and with his stripes we are healed.

ISAIAH 53:5

Then shall thy light break forth as the morning, and thine health shall spring forth speedily: and thy righteousness shall go before thee; the glory of the LORD shall be thy reward.

ISAIAH 58:8

For I will restore health unto thee, and I will heal thee of thy wounds, saith the Lord; because they called thee an Outcast, saying, this is Zion, whom no man seeketh after.

JEREMIAH 30:17

These signs shall follow them that believe ... they shall lay hands on the sick, and they shall recover.

MARK 16:17, 18

How God anointed Jesus of Nazareth with the Holy Ghost and power: who went about doing good, and healing all that were oppressed of the devil; for God was with him.

ACTS 10:38

Jesus Christ the same yesterday, and today, and for ever. HEBREWS 13:8

Is any sick among you? let him call for the elders of the church; and let them pray over him, anointing him with oil in the name of the Lord; And the prayer of faith shall save the sick, and the Lord shall raise him up; and if he have committed sins, they shall be forgiven him.

JAMES 5:14, 15

Chapter Twelve

How to Cope With Sorrow,
Bereavement and Broken Hearts

I have been a minister for over 30 years now, and part of my God-given task is to help people meet sorrow when it comes. I too have suffered sorrow, so I can empathize with those who come to me for counsel.

Some years ago, I lost three loved ones in the course of a single month. First a dear friend and man of God who had been a great inspiration to my life was senselessly killed in an auto accident. Everyone in the other car was drunk.

Next, an aunt whom I loved dearly was killed in another highway crash. This was quite a blow, for my aunt and I had been very close.

Then a call came from my friend Don Olson, telling me that he was accompanying the body of his brother, Virgil, back to Seattle. Virgil had been killed by carbon monoxide fumes while on the bus of the famous Blackwood Brothers Gospel Quartet. Just the day before, I'd seen and talked with Virgil in Vancouver. He'd been strong and healthy. His brother Don was devastated as he talked with me on the phone. I did my best to help him in his grief, but it was hard for me to come to grips with Virgil's death myself. It seemed such a loss: Virgil had been only 30, and he left behind a wife and three young children. It was enough to break your heart.

Do you have a broken heart? In my ministry I have met many whose hearts have been broken. Perhaps it was caused by a sudden bereavement, a divorce, separation from loved ones, unrequited love, the loss of a job, the loss of friends, an unfaithful mate, a prodigal son or daughter.

Sometimes even good things can cause heartbreak, as when a son or daughter receives a call to foreign missions and moves to the other side of the globe.

Other times, bad things "work together for good" in the plan of God. I'm thinking of times when men have lost jobs only to find better ones; times when engagements have been broken and the one who was so heartbroken at the time ended up marrying a far better mate in the course of time.

Friends, whatever the cause of your sorrow, Jesus said, "Let not your heart be troubled." I know that there are experiences — especially the death of a loved one — that can come near shattering the human spirit. It is as though a beacon light suddenly goes out, leaving the bereaved person to wander across a desolate plain from which every familiar guiding landmark seems to have been obliterated. To lose a loved one seems so absolute and final, that no matter how well-adjusted you may try to be, the loss seems almost too much to bear.

I want to share with you some practical advice on how to face sorrow and live through it with fortitude. I do not wish to offer some glib theory or formula on how to overcome the overwhelming pain of bereavement or heartache. For those of you who have been bereaved of a loved one, or who have suffered some other overwhelming loss, I offer to you the same consolation that has ministered to me and countless others who have been in the same situation. Because it has worked for us, I believe it will work for you.

When life seems bereft of hope and we lack even the courage to face another day, one thing towers above all the rest like a great mountain above the lesser foothills. I am speaking of faith. When we face unbearable sorrow, it is faith in God, faith in His Word, faith in His infinite goodness that will enable us to cope.

In the final analysis, when we receive Jesus, we receive life: abundant life, everlasting life. The Bible says in John 1:4, "In him was life; and the life was the light of men." Christianity is life contrasted with death; it is hope contrasted with despair; it is victory contrasted with defeat. Christianity is the most radiant, vital, dynamic force ever to come into human history.

When we face sorrow, we need to remember that what we face right here, right now, is only momentary compared to the vastness of all eternity — and that we are going to live forever. Our bodies may die, but we will live on. Several thousand years from now, the thing that will be important is not the loss that seems so overwhelming now. The thing that will count for all eternity is not what happens to us, but how we cope with the trials that come.

We know that we will live on after death because Jesus said, "I am the resurrection and the life: he that believeth in Me, though he were dead, yet shall he live: whosoever liveth and believeth in Me shall never die" (John 11:25). At the Last Supper, Jesus said, "Because I live, ye shall live also" (John 14:19). Then He removed all doubt by dying on the Cross and rising from the dead. In that moment, was established the bedrock of our Christian faith: the supreme fact that Jesus, whom death could not kill, still lives; and that through faith in Him we too are destined to live on as spiritual beings in a spiritual world on the far side of death.

Very often people who come close to dying report that they have encountered sights or sounds that certainly do not seem to belong to this world. I have been at the bedside of dear Christians who have told of the lights they have seen, or the music they have heard — not music as we know it here, but music of indescribable sweetness and harmony.

Some winters ago, my friend William Freeman and I were in a devastating car wreck. The big Buick we were in struck black ice on the highway, left the road, went over an embankment and rolled over and over. I escaped injury, but Brother Freeman was nearly killed. For 106 hours he lay in a coma; then, when it seemed he had gone from this life, the Lord God came and spoke to him, "I want to show you how easy death is for a Christian."

Next, Brother Freeman told me, he was caught up out of his body and was transported across valleys, hills, mountains, and rivers, until finally he reached what he described as "the crossing river." There he beheld the glories of a realm far exceeding anything of this life. Just before he entered that glorious place forever, the Lord turned him around and sent him back to this earth. Thereafter, Brother Freeman often told me about the wonder it was to face death as a Christian.

The testimonies of Christians who have been brought back from the brink of death should give us all enormous comfort as we face bereavement. Death, however, is just one of life's many sorrows. But whatever the cause of your grief, I have good news. Jesus is just as concerned about broken hearts as He is about broken bodies: He came to heal both.

When Jesus returned from His temptation in the wilderness, He entered a synagogue on the Sabbath day and there proclaimed: "The Spirit of the Lord is upon me, because he hath anointed me to preach the gospel to the poor; he hath sent me to heal the broken-hearted (Luke 4:18). Psalm 34:18 says, "The Lord is nigh unto them that are of a broken heart; and saveth such as be of a contrite spirit." And Psalm 147:3 confirms, "He healeth the broken in heart, and bindeth up their wounds."

There have been several times my heart has been near breaking — when my only brother was dying, when I lost friends and other loved ones, when my wife nearly died after a miscarriage, and even when my sons left home for gospel work in Far East Asia. Each time, I found that Jesus was the answer. "From the end of the earth will I cry unto thee, when my heart is overwhelmed: lead me to the rock that is higher than I" (Psalm 61:2).

Have you been bereaved? Is your heart broken? Remember that God is "The God of all comfort; Who comforteth us in all our tribulation, that we may be able to comfort them which are in any trouble, by the comfort wherewith we ourselves are comforted of God" (2 Corinthians 1:3, 4).

"Now our Lord Jesus Christ himself, and God, even our Father, which hath loved us, and hath given us everlasting consolation and good hope through grace, Comfort your hearts, and establish you in every good word and work" (2 Thessalonians 2:16, 17).

RX for Action:

Do you want truth that will minister comfort, strength and assurance right now? Stop and affirm aloud the 23rd Psalm.

Promises for the Brokenhearted

While God sometimes pours out His blessings in a sovereign manner, most times we have to pray and ask Him for them. You didn't get saved automatically: you had to ask. Most of us didn't get baptized in the Holy Spirit automatically, either: we had to pray and ask God for this experience. Physical healing and emotional healings come in a similar manner: we find a Scripture that meets our needs, then we pray and believe that God will cause His Word to come to pass in our lives. Here are some Scriptures to stand on when you need God's comfort:

Blessed are they that mourn; for they shall be comforted.

MATTHEW 5:4

And he said, While the child was yet alive, I fasted and wept: for I said, Who can tell whether GOD will be gracious to me, that the child may live? But now he is dead, wherefore should I fast? can I bring him back again? I shall go to him, but he shall not return to me.

2 SAMUEL 12:22, 23

And they that know thy name will put their trust in thee: for thou, LORD, hast not forsaken them that seek thee.

PSALM 9:10

When my father and my mother forsake me, then the LORD will take me up.

PSALM 27:10

Precious in the sight of the LORD is the death of his saints.

PSALM 116:15

The righteous perisheth, and no man layeth it to heart: and merciful men are taken away, none considering that the righteous is taken away from the evil to come.

ISAIAH 57:1

The spirit of the Lord GOD is upon me; because the LORD hath anointed me to preach good tidings unto the meek; he hath sent me to bind up the brokenhearted, to proclaim liberty to the captives, and the opening of the prison to them that are bound; To proclaim the acceptable year of the LORD, and the day of vengeance of our God; to comfort all that mourn; To appoint unto them that mourn in Zion, to give unto them beauty for ashes, the oil of joy for mourning, the garment of praise for the spirit of heaviness; that they might be called trees of righteousness, the planting of the LORD, that he might be glorified.

ISAIAH 61:1-3

Verily, verily, I say unto you, That ye shall weep and lament, but the world shall rejoice: and ye shall be sorrowful, but your sorrow shall be turned into joy. A woman when she is in travail hath sorrow, because her hour is come: but as soon as she is delivered of the child, she remembereth no more the anguish, for joy that a man is born into the world.

JOHN 16:20-22

O death, where is thy sting? O grave, where is thy victory? The sting of death is sin: and the strength of sin is the law. But thanks be to God, which giveth us the victory through our Lord Jesus Christ.

1 CORINTHIANS 15:55-57

For we have not an high priest which cannot be touched with the feeling of our infirmities; but was in all points tempted like as we are, yet without sin. Let us therefore come boldly unto the throne of grace, that we may obtain mercy, and find grace to help in time of need.

HEBREWS 4:15, 16

Chapter Thirteen

How to Cope
With Enemies

When the prophet Ezra and his companions left Babylon to return to Jerusalem, they witnessed God's deliverance from their enemies. "We departed from the river of Ahava on the twelfth day of the first month, to go unto Jerusalem: and the hand of our God was upon us, and he delivered us from the hand of the enemy, and of such as lay in wait by the way" (Ezra 8:31).

January 12, 1971, proved to be a decisive day for Joyce and me. It was the first time in our lives that we had ever been in court. An enemy of the gospel had pressed eight charges against us.

A Christian lawyer handled our case without charge, and after a fiery 80-minute court session, we too could testify with Ezra that "the hand of our God was upon us, and he delivered us from the hand of the enemy." The judge dropped all eight charges, and the case was dismissed.

Christians, especially, need to know how to cope with enemies, for Jesus said, "Woe unto you, when all men shall speak well of you! for so did their fathers to the false prophets" (Luke 6:26). As Christians, we can expect to be hated by those who are not believers, for Jesus said, "If ye were of the world, the world would love his own: but because ye are not of the world, but I have chosen you out of the world, therefore the world hateth you" (John 15:19). Yet I have heard Christians say, "I haven't an enemy in the world."

Usually, someone who would boast that he has no enemies is either incredibly naive or regrettably insincere. Even without the spiritual forces at work in the world today, it's nearly impossible to pass through life without making an enemy somewhere along the way.

Jesus commanded us to love and pray for our enemies. He said, "Love your enemies, bless them that curse you, do good to them that hate you, and pray for them which despitefully use you, and persecute you" (Matthew 5:44). Jesus lived this way himself. He demonstrated this kind of love on the Cross when He said, "Father, forgive them; for they know not what they do" (Luke 23:34).

Stephen also demonstrated this forgiving attitude toward his enemies when, dying from the stones hurled at him by an angry mob, he prayed, "Lord, lay not this sin to their charge" (Acts 7:60).

The Bible tells us to offer our enemies kindness when we have the opportunity: "Therefore if thine enemy hunger, feed him; if he thirst, give him drink: for in so doing thou shalt heap coals of fire on his head. Be not overcome of evil, but overcome evil with good" (Romans 12:20, 21).

David overcame his enemy, King Saul, not by the sword but by kindness. "Then said Saul, I have sinned: return, my son David: for I will no more do thee harm, because my soul was precious in thine eyes this day: behold, I have played the fool, and have erred exceedingly" (1 Samuel 26:21). "A soft answer turneth away wrath: but grievous words stir up anger" (Proverbs 15:1).

Would you like for your enemies to be at peace with you? The Scriptures tell us how this can be accomplished. "When a man's ways please the Lord, he maketh even his enemies to be at peace with him" (Proverbs 16:7).

When Joyce and I were delivered from our court case, we claimed Psalm 41:1-3: "Blessed is he that considereth the poor: the Lord will deliver him in time of trouble. The Lord will preserve him, and keep him alive; and he shall be blessed upon the earth: and thou wilt not deliver him unto the will of his enemies. The Lord will strengthen him upon the bed of languishing: thou wilt make all his bed in his sickness."

God promises that as we consider the poor and minister the gospel to them, we shall be blessed, delivered in time of trouble, preserved from an untimely death, delivered from the will of enemies, strengthened when languishing, and healed of sickness. If you are considering the poor, if you are giving unselfishly so that the poor of the earth may hear the gospel, then you can claim God's deliverance this day and every day.

David prayed for deliverance from his enemies, and I believe that it is scriptural for us to pray for deliverance from ours as well. "Deliver me from my enemies, O my God: defend me from them that rise up against me" (Psalm 59:1). "Hear my voice, O God, in my prayer: preserve my life from fear of the enemy" (Psalm 64:1).

God specializes in delivering His children from their enemies. "And the Lord ... delivered you out of the hand of your enemies on every side, and ye dwelled safe" (1 Samuel 12:11). "He delivereth me from mine enemies: yea, thou liftest me up above those that rise up against me: thou hast delivered me from the violent man" (Psalm 18:48).

It is all-important, to keep the right heart attitude toward those who do us wrong. When God delivers you, praise God for your deliverance — but don't rejoice at anything bad that may have happened to your enemy. "O give thanks unto the Lord; for he is good: for his mercy endureth for ever ... [he] hath redeemed us from our enemies" (Psalm 136:1, 24). "Rejoice not when thine enemy falleth, and let not thine heart be glad when he stumbleth: Lest the LORD see it, and it displease him, and he turn away his wrath from him" (Proverbs 24:17, 18).

In coping with enemies, it is all-important for our own spiritual well-being that we maintain a forgiving attitude. A forgiving spirit is an absolute necessity if we hope to live a victorious Christian life. Jesus said, "If ye forgive men their trespasses, your heavenly Father will also forgive you. But if ye forgive not men their trespasses, neither will your Father forgive your trespasses (Matthew 6:14, 15).

According to the words of Jesus, the failure to forgive can have serious consequences. If you are holding unforgiveness in your heart, God will not forgive YOUR sins. And we all have sins: "If we say that we have no sin, we deceive ourselves, and the truth is not in us" (1 John 1:8). Therefore, our own unforgiveness will cut us off from fellowship with God and make our praying ineffective — for it is only the "effectual fervent prayer of a RIGHTEOUS [i.e., forgiven] man" which "availeth much" (James 5:16).

We all possess the power to forgive. God would not require the impossible of us. God's ability within us to forgive others is unlimited. Jesus said we should be willing to forgive "seventy times seven." This is not a natural ability, but a supernatural ability with which God enables us to forgive others.

What is the secret to forgiving others freely? This secret is found in one word: LOVE. God gives us the ability to love with His love, to see others through His eyes of tenderness and compassion. "The love of God is shed abroad in our hearts by the Holy Ghost which is given unto us" (Romans 5:5).

Ephesians 4:32 says, "And be ye kind one to another, tenderhearted, forgiving one another, even as God for Christ's sake hath forgiven you." Kindness is a fruit of the Spirit (Galatians 5:22). When coupled with tenderheartedness, it enables you to forgive.

Some say, "I would forgive others if they would only ask for forgiveness." Whether they ask for your forgiveness or not, you can and should forgive them, for the sake of your own spiritual well-being. Otherwise, leave yourself open to what Hebrews 12:15 calls a "root of bitterness": "Looking diligently, lest any man fail of the grace of God; lest any root of bitterness springing up trouble you, and thereby many be defiled."

Unforgiveness leads to bitterness, and bitterness defiles. Instead, purpose now to forgive. Refuse to speak unkindly against those who have wronged you. God will enable you to forgive and to forget.

RX for Action:

Remember that God's Word reveals that Christians will ALWAYS have enemies.

The Scripture doesn't say "we wrestle not"; it says "we wrestle not AGAINST FLESH AND BLOOD" (Ephesians 6:12). The person coming against you is not your real enemy: your real enemy is the demonic force that motivates him to do what he is doing. So RESIST the devil, but LOVE and FORGIVE the person he is victimizing.

Purpose to maintain a forgiving attitude. Do not allow a "root of bitterness" to take hold.

Coping With Enemies

God promises to protect us from our enemies, but He insists that we love and forgive them. Here are some scriptures to claim in the areas of protection and forgiveness:

For the LORD your God is he that goeth with you, to fight for you against your enemies, to save you.

DEUTERONOMY 20:4

The LORD shall cause thine enemies that rise up against thee to be smitten before thy face: they shall come out against thee one way, and flee before thee seven ways.

DEUTERONOMY 28:7

He will keep the feet of his saints, and the wicked shall be silent in darkness; for by strength shall no man prevail.

1 SAMUEL 2:9

The LORD executeth righteousness and judgment for all that are oppressed.

PSALM 103:6

Say not thou, I will recompense evil; but wait on the LORD, and he shall save thee.

PROVERBS 20:22

If thine enemy be hungry, give him bread to eat; and if he be thirsty, give him water to drink: For thou shalt heap coals of fire upon his head, and the LORD shall reward thee.

PROVERBS 25:21, 22

Blessed are they which are persecuted for righteousness' sake: for theirs is the kingdom of heaven. Blessed are ye, when men shall revile you, and persecute you, and shall say all manner of evil against you falsely, for my sake. Rejoice, and be exceeding glad: for great is your reward in heaven: for so persecuted they the prophets which were before you.

MATTHEW 5:10-12

But I say unto you. Love your enemies, bless them that curse you, do good to them that hate you, and pray for them which despitefully use you, and persecute you; That ye may be the children of your Father which is in heaven ...

MATTHEW 5:44, 45

These things I have spoken unto you, that in me ye might have peace. In the world ye shall have tribulations: but be of good cheer; I have overcome the world.

JOHN 16:33

Bless them which persecute you: bless, and curse not.

ROMANS 12:14

Let all bitterness, and wrath, and anger, and clamour, and evil speaking, be put away from you, with all malice: And be ye kind one to another, tenderhearted, forgiving one another, even as God for Christ's sake hath forgiven you.

EPHESIANS 4:31, 32

Put on therefore, as the elect of God, holy and beloved, bowels of mercies, kindness, humbleness of mind, meekness, longsuffering; Forbearing one another, and forgiving one another, if any man have a quarrel against any: even as Christ forgave you, so also do ye. And above all these things put on charity, which is the bond of perfectness.

COLOSSIANS 3:12-14

Beloved, think it not strange concerning the fiery trial which is to try you, as though some strange thing happened unto you: But rejoice, inasmuch as ye are partakers of Christ's sufferings; that, when his glory shall be revealed, ye may be glad also with exceeding joy. If ye be reproached for the name of Christ, happy are ye; for the spirit of glory and of God resteth upon you: on their part he is evil spoken of, but on your part he is glorified.

1 PETER 4: 12-14

Chapter Fourteen

How to Cope
With Gambling

Gambling was a big part of my dad's sinful life when I was growing up as a young man. It was the source of a lot of heartache to our family, even without all the losses Dad experienced. He actually operated a gambling hall where men often lost their fortunes at the gaming table.

I grew up with a very close-hand observation of the perils of gambling, and I want to share with you my feelings concerning it.

There are many different kinds of gambling. Some, like Russian roulette, are obviously satanic. Others less flagrantly sinful. Some people ask me "What about bingo games and lotteries?" These may appear quite innocent; so much so, that you sometimes see them conducted in denominational churches. Oftentimes, they are used to help promote a "good cause." But I believe any kind of gambling is a sin.

Let me give you reasons why gambling is wrong:

1. Gambling promotes a greedy spirit. It emphasizes "getting" rather than "giving." Selfish interest is the

important factor, instead of a self-sacrificial life. As Christians, our motivation is "I live to give." Gambling erodes the moral fiber of our lives.

2. Gambling promotes a lazy spirit. It de-emphasizes the Protestant work ethic. But the Bible says "Wealth gotten by vanity shall be diminished: but he that gathereth by labour shall increase" (Proverbs 13:11).

3. Gambling puts faith in chance or luck, rather than the care and provisions of our Heavenly Father.

4. The person who gambles seeks to profit from the loss to someone else, yet the Bible says, "Give to him that asketh thee, and from him that would borrow of thee turn not thou away" (Matthew 5:42).

5. Gambling is addictive. There are many who would stop if they could; but they cannot. This is because an evil spirit has them in its grasp and they need deliverance. Just as some men drink without becoming alcoholics, some men gamble without becoming gamblers. But the more gambling is indulged in, the more likely it is that the kind of evil spirit that causes some to be addicted to this vice will find a foothold.

Gambling is not for Christians. There are other ways by which a Christian can gain materially. Some of these are:

1. Work. "If any would not work, neither should he eat" (2 Thessalonians 3:10).

2. Wise investment. Read "The Parable of the Pounds" in Luke 19:1-27.

3. Gift or inheritance. "Children ought not to lay up for their parents, but the parents for their children" (2 Corinthians 12:14).

Billy Graham once said:

> The appeal of gambling is somewhat understandable. There is something about getting "something for nothing." I realize that, and that is where the sin lies.
>
> Gambling of any kind amounts to "theft by permission." The coin is flipped, the dice is rolled or the horse is run, and somebody rakes in what belongs to another. The Bible says, "In the sweat of thy face shalt thou eat bread" (Genesis 3:19). It doesn't say, "By the flip of a coin, shalt thou eat thy lunch!"
>
> I realize that in most petty gambling, no harm is intended. But the principle is the same as in big gambling. The difference is only in the amount of money involved.

The Apostle Paul warned, "Abstain from all appearance of evil" (1 Thessalonians 5:22). I believe that this means we shouldn't even play at gambling. In other words, no poker games — even when you play only for chips and no money is involved.

How can you cope with gambling? Extreme cases will need to seek a Spirit-filled pastor for deliverance. But most of us can cope with it simply by realizing the authority of God's Word:

Exodus 20:15, 17 "Thou shalt not steal ... Thou shalt not covet thy neighbour's house. Thou shalt not covet ... anything that is thy neighbour's."

Colossians 3:2, 5-6, "Set your affection on things above, not on things on the earth ... Mortify therefore your members which are upon the earth; fornication, uncleanness, inordinate affection, evil concupiscence, and covetousness, which is idolatry: For which things' sake, the wrath of God cometh on the children of disobedience."

The standard for all of our activities is revealed in 1 Corinthians 10:31, "Whether therefore you eat, or drink, or whatsoever ye do, do all to the glory of God." And 1 Corinthians 6:12, "All things are lawful unto me, but all things are not expedient; all things are lawful for me, but I will not be brought under the power of any."

Sometimes, the temptation to gamble comes because people are struggling with piles of bills, wondering how they are going to maintain themselves and their families. If you have read the preceding chapters, you must realize by now that the Word of God promises prosperity to those who will obey the teachings of the Bible.

Philippians 4:19 has been my battle cry for 35 years in the full-time ministry: "But my God shall supply all your need according to his riches in glory by Christ Jesus."

Do you need a financial miracle? Proclaim Philippians 4:19 aloud. Say, "God has promised to supply all my need according to His riches in glory by Christ Jesus!"

However, we always have to be fair to the entire context of this passage in Philippians 4. These words were addressed to people who were bountiful, cheerful givers.

The Bible makes it clear that we are stewards of our money. Money is a gift of God, and it is to be used for

His glory. If our money is squandered selfishly or employed greedily, it brings misery and distress upon those who possess it.

It is not money that is the root of all evil, but the *love* of money. When money is invested and shared for the glory of God, it can be a boon and a blessing; not only to us, but to those who receive our love gifts.

The Bible clearly teaches that all our money belongs to God. The Bible suggest that our giving should be a tithe as a minimum response in gratitude to God for His provisions. The Scriptures promise both spiritual and material blessings to the one who gives to the Lord.

It may be a cliché, but it's very true that "you can't out-give God." In fact, if we give to God bountifully, He will give to us bountifully. If we give to Him stingily, that is how He will return it to us. "Give, and it shall be given unto you; good measure, pressed down, and shaken together, and running over, shall men give into your bosom. For WITH THE SAME MEASURE that you mete withal it shall be measured to you again" (Luke 6:38). And, "But this I say, He which soweth sparingly shall reap also sparingly; and he which soweth bountifully shall reap also bountifully" (2 Corinthians 9:6).

It's not enough, in endeavoring to cope with financial difficulties, to talk about the stewardship of money without probing gently to discover some causes of financial problems. For some people it's drinking, gambling, and sinful living. But many of us need to examine our Christian lifestyles, to see if it's our own over-spending that is causing the problem.

After we have asked God to search our hearts on the matter, if we discover there are no barriers in our own practice with our money that causes our difficulties, then we also need to realize that Satan himself can be hindering our blessings from coming to us, just as he did in Job's life. However, as New Testament believers, we have the authority to rebuke and bind the devil in the name of Jesus, to plead the power of the blood of Jesus over our lives, and to offer praise and thanksgiving to God for the blessings that are now on their way. It is also important to seek God's will for His direction concerning how we should handle and spend the money we do have.

As a husband, a father of five children, and a faith minister for 35 years, I have probably had as many experiences in coping with financial difficulties as any area this book presents. But I take great confidence in the fact of the Father's provision.

RX FOR ACTION:

To cope with gambling, first recognize it for what it is — a sin.

Use the Word of God to "crucify the flesh" in this area.

If you have become addicted to gambling to the point where you are out of control, seek prayer from a Spirit-filled minister or other mature believer. "Confess your faults one to another, and pray one for another, that ye may be healed. The effectual fervent prayer of a righteous man availeth much" (James 5:16).

Realize that there are ways for Christians to acquire wealth. Pay your tithes, give your offerings, and seek God for His wisdom concerning your financial situation.

How to Keep From Being Possessed by Your Possessions

Although it is God's desire that we enjoy prosperity (3 John 2), it is displeasing to Him when we allow our prosperity to get in the way of our service to Him. The very thing which was meant to be a blessing can become a hindrance, a roadblock on our journey to heaven.

There is a way, however, to keep our possessions from possessing us:

Ten Commandments About Money

1. Thou shalt remember that money has its limitations. It can buy everything but happiness. It can buy a ticket to every place but heaven. "Thy money perish with thee, because thou hast thought that the gift of God may be purchased with money" (Acts 8:20).

2. Thou shalt not let prosperity cause thee to forget God. Deuteronomy 8:11-20 warns that when your possessions are multiplied, you must not forget God.

3. Thou shalt remember that the love of money is the root of all evil. "For the love of money is the root of all evil: which while some coveted after, they have erred

from the faith, and pierced themselves through with many sorrows" (2 Timothy 6:10).

4. Thou shalt acknowledge all things belong to God. "The silver is mine, and the gold is mine, saith the Lord" (Haggai 2:8)

5. Thou shalt admit God giveth thee power to obtain possessions. "Charge them that are rich in this world, that they be not highminded, nor trust in uncertain riches, but in the living God, who giveth us richly all things to enjoy" (1 Timothy 6:17).

7. Thou shalt not set thine heart upon riches. "If riches increase, set not your heart upon them" (Psalm 62:10).

8. Thou shalt not boast of thine ability in obtaining riches. We are warned not to say, "My power and the might of mine hand have gotten me this wealth" (Deuteronomy 8:17).

9. Thou shalt not glory in thy possessions. "Thus saith the LORD, let not the wise man glory in his wisdom, neither let the mighty man glory in his might, let not the rich man glory in his riches" (Jeremiah 9:23).

10. Thou shalt devote thy possessions to God's service. "But God said unto him, Thou fool, this night thy soul shall be required of thee: then whose shall those things be, which thou hast provided? So is he that layeth

up treasure for himself, and is not rich toward God"
(Luke 12: 20-21).

Money Will Buy

A bed, but not sleep.
Books, but not brains.
Finery, but not beauty.
A house, but not a home.
Medicine, but not health.
Luxuries, but not culture.
Amusements, but not happiness.
A crucifix, but not a Saviour.
A church pew, but not heaven.

— Pilgrim Holiness Advocate

Closing Words

In March, 1985, I was conducting an open air crusade in Madurai, India. Madurai was the original capital of India, later replaced by Delhi. One day I was invited to speak at the Central Prison of Madurai.

The warden, a Spirit-filled Christian, had made all the arrangements for my prison ministry that day. He met me outside the prison walls and escorted me and my team through the gates.

It was an unforgettable experience to be met by the uniformed guards, who snapped their rifles in rhythmic military style as we approached them. Then I was introduced to the superintendent, a tall stately man who had been keenly influenced by the old days of the British rule in India.

As we walked briskly to the prison chapel, I was informed that 1,295 prisoners were awaiting my visit. Of that number, 550 of the men were convicted murderers who would either be hanged on the gallows, or would spend their life sentences in prison.

"Lord," I prayed, "how do I cope with 550 convicted murderers? What do I say to them?"

When we reached the chapel, I was introduced to speak to the men. All of them were seated on the floor. I deliberately made eye contact with each row of men, going from man to man, looking directly at them.

Compassion gripped my heart as I thought of these men and their sentences because of crimes they had committed.

After I preached a fervent salvation message, I gave the Savior's invitation for men to receive Christ. The response was immediate and wide-spread throughout the chapel.

Then the assistant warden walked up to me to ask if I would pray for the sick.

"Many men have diseases and would like for you to pray for them," he advised me.

Readily, I assured him I would lay hands upon each man who desired my prayers.

I was asked if I would like to go down onto the chapel floor to pray for the men.

I surveyed the situation, noting there were guards situated throughout the chapel. The Holy Spirit dropped into my heart a word of wisdom: "Bring the men to the platform so that all may witness the love of Christ."

As those prisoners filed across that platform, I laid hands upon them and invoked the name of Jesus against their infirmities.

I looked deep into their eyes, conveying the love of Christ to them in every genuine way possible. It was an experience in compassionate faith that was to reach and touch hundreds of lives that morning.

After all the prisoners had received ministry, I was asked to lay my hands upon the guards and pray for them. Next came the warden and his assistant.

Finally, the stately superintendent stepped forward and requested my prayers. (Later, the Christian warden was exuberant as he said, "That was one of the biggest miracles of all ... the superintendent was neither Christian nor Hindu ... he was an avowed atheist!" Until that morning!)

When I returned home from that mission, it marked my 61st overseas missionary journey into 31 nations. Learning how to cope with people in so many nations with their cultural differences has been lessons in living the principles I have set forth in this book.

Even as I have prepared this manuscript, new experiences in coping have come across my pathway.

My wife, Joyce, has often asked me, "Does your book really have practical answers, or is it just so much religious jargon?"

It does have answers.

But her questions have probed my spirit, causing me to examine and re-examine what I have written.

I pray that after reading this book, you will be better able to cope with your problems, circumstances, challenges and needs by applying these positive principles of God's Word.

More Faith-Building Books

America Betrayed! by Marlin Maddoux. This hard-hitting book exposes the forces in our country which seek to destroy the family, the schools and our values. This book details exactly how the news media manipulates your mind. Marlin Maddoux is the host of the popular, national radio talk show "Point of View."

A Reasonable Reason to Wait, by Jacob Aranza, is a frank, definitive discussion on premarital sex — from the biblical viewpoint. God speaks specifically about premarital sex, according to the author. The Bible also provides a healing message for those who have already been sexually involved before marriage. This book is a must reading for every young person — and also for parents — who really want to known the biblical truth on this important subject.

Backward Masking Unmasked, by Jacob Aranza. Rock'n'Roll music affects tens of millions of young people and adults in America and around the world. This music is laced with lyrics exalting drugs, the occult, immorality, homosexuality, violence and rebellion. But there is more sinister danger in this music according to the author. It's called "backward masking." Numerous rock groups employ this mind-influencing technique in their recordings. Teenagers by the millions — who spend hours each day listening to rock music — aren't even aware the messages are there. The author clearly exposes these dangers.

Backward Masking Unmasked, (cassette tape) by Jacob Aranza. Hear actual satanic messages and judge for yourself.

Beast, by Dan Betzer. This is the story of the rise to power of the future world dictator — the antichrist. This novel plots a dark web of intrigue which begins with the suicide-death of Adolf Hitler who believed he had been chosen to be the world dictator. Yet, in his last days, he spoke of "the man who will come after me." Several decades later that man, Jacque Catroux, head of the European economic system, appears on the world scene. He had been born the day Hitler died, conceived by the seed of Lucifer himself. In articulate prose, the author describes the "disappearance" of the Christians from the earth; the horror and hopelessness which followed that event; and the bitter agony of life on earth after all moral and spiritual restraints are removed.

Devil Take the Youngest by Winkie Pratney. This book reveals the war on children that is being waged in America and the world today. Pratney, a world-renowned author, teacher and conference speaker, says there is a spirit of Moloch loose in the land. The author relates distinct parallels of the ancient worship of Moloch — where little children were sacrificed screaming into his burning fire — to the tragic killing and kidnapping of children today. This timely book says the war on children has its roots in the occult.

Globalism: America's Demise, by William Bowen, Jr. The Globalists — some of the most powerful people on earth — have plans to totally eliminate God, the family, and the United States as we know it today. Globalism is the vehicle humanists are using to implement their secular humanistic philosophy to bring about their one-world government. The four goals of Globalism are 1) a one-world government 2) a new world religion 3) a new economic system 4) a new race of people for the new world order. This book alerts Christians to what Globalists have planned for them.

Hearts on Fire, by Jimmy Phillips. What is God doing throughout the world? Where is revival taking place? What is the heart's cry of the people? Jimmy Phillips answers these and other important questions in this delightful book. During his travels as a missionary-evangelist, Jimmy Phillips has ministered both in the rag cities of India and the largest church in the world which is in

Korea. As you read his story, your heart will be set on fire as you take a fresh look at the world through his eyes.

More Rock, Country & Back Masking Unmasked by Jacob Aranza. Aranza's first book, *Backward Masking Unmasked* was a national bestseller. It clearly exposed the backward satanic messages included in a lot of rock and roll music. Now, in the sequel, Aranza gives a great deal of new information on backward messages. Also, for the first time in Christian literature, he takes a hard look at the content, meaning and dangers of country music. "Rock, though filled with satanism, sex and drugs ... has a hard time keeping up with the cheatin', drinkin' and one-night stands that continue to dominate country music," the author says.

Murdered Heiress ... Living Witness, by Dr. Petti Wagner. The victim of a sinister kidnapping and murder plot, the Lord miraculously gave her life back to her. Dr. Wagner — heiress to a large fortune — was kidnapped, tortured, beaten, electrocuted and died. A doctor signed her death certificate, yet she lives today!

Natalie — The Miracle Child by Barry and Cathy Beaver. This is the heartwarming, inspirational story of little Natalie Beaver — God's miracle child — who was born with virtually no chance to live — until God intervened! When she was born her internal organs were outside her body. The doctors said she would never survive. Yet, God performed a miracle and Natalie is healed today. Now, as a pre-teen, she is a gifted singer and sings the praises of a miracle-working God.

Rest From the Quest, by Elissa Lindsey McClain. This is the candid account of a former New Ager who spent the first 29 years of her life in the New Age Movement, the occult and Eastern mysticism. This is an incredible inside look at what really goes on in the New Age Movement.

The Hidden Dangers of the Rainbow, by Constance Cumbey. A national #1 bestseller, this is a vivid exposé of the New Age Movement which is dedicated to wiping out Christianity and establishing a one-world order. This movement — a vest network of tens of thousands of occultic and other organizations — meets the test of prophecy concerning the Antichrist.

The Hidden Dangers of the Rainbow Tape, by Constance Cumbey. Mrs. Cumbey, a trial lawyer from Detroit, Michigan, gives inside information on the New Age Movement in this teaching tape.

The Miracle of Touching, by Dr. John Hornbrook. Most everyone enjoys the special attention that a loving touch brings. Throughout the chapters of this encouraging book the author explains what touching others through love — under the careful guidance of the Lord Jesus Christ — can accomplish. Dr. Hornbrook urges Christians to reach out and touch someone — family members, friends, prisoners — and do it to the glory of God, physically, emotionally and spiritually.

The Twisted Cross, by Joseph Carr. One of the most important works of our decade, The Twisted Cross clearly documents the occult and demonic influence on Adolf Hitler and the Third Reich which led to the Holocaust killing of more than six million Jews. The author even gives the specifics of the bizarre way in which Hitler actually became demon-possessed.

Who Will Rise Up? by Jed Smock. This is the incredible — and sometimes hilarious — story of Jed Smock, who with his wife, Cindy, has preached the uncompromising gospel on the malls and lawns of hundreds of university campuses throughout this land. They have been mocked, rocked, stoned, mobbed, beaten, jailed, cursed and ridiculed by the students. Yet this former university professor and his wife have seen the miracle-working power of God transform thousands of lives on university campuses.

Yes, send me the following books:

___ copy (copies) of **America Betrayed!** @ $5.95
___ copy (copies) of **A Reasonable Reason To Wait** @ $4.95
___ copy (copies) of **Backward Masking Unmasked** @ $4.95
___ copy (copies) of **Backward Masking Unmasked Cassette Tape** @ $5.95
___ copy (copies) of **Beast** @ $5.95
___ copy (copies) of **Devil Take the Youngest** @ $6.95
___ copy (copies) of **Globalism: America's Demise** @ $6.95
___ copy (copies) of **God's Timetable for the 1980's** @ $5.95
___ copy (copies) of **Hearts on Fire** @ $5.95
___ copy (copies) of **How to Cope When You Can't** @ $5.95
___ copy (copies) of **More Rock, Country & Backward Masking Unmasked** @ $5.95
___ copy (copies) of **Murdered Heiress . . . Living Witness** @ $5.95
___ copy (copies) of **Natalie** @ $4.95
___ copy (copies) of **Rest From the Quest** @ $5.95
___ copy (copies) of **Take Him to the Streets** @ $6.95
___ copy (copies) of **The Agony of Deception** @ $6.95
___ copy (copies) of **The Divine Connection** @ $4.95
___ copy (copies) of **The Hidden Dangers of the Rainbow** @ $5.95
___ copy (copies) of **The Hidden Dangers of the Rainbow Seminar Tapes** @ $19.95
___ copy (copies) of **The Miracle of Touching** @ $5.95
___ copy (copies) of **The Twisted Cross** @ $7.95
___ copy (copies) of **Who Will Rise Up?** @ $5.95

AT BOOKSTORES EVERYWHERE or order direct from Huntington House, Inc., P.O. Box 53788, Lafayette, LA 70505

Send check/money order or, for faster service VISA/Mastercard orders call toll-free 1-800-572-8213. Add: Freight and handling, $1.00 for the first book ordered, 50¢ for each additional book.

Enclosed is $ _____ including postage.

Name _____

Address _____

City _____ State and ZIP _____